Ambassador of God

1 A Man of the Holy Spirit

Ambassador of God

1 A Man of the Holy Spirit

2nd edition, 1st printing, November 2013
Published by Duranno Press
Phone : +82-2-2078-3444
Email : rights@duranno.com
Home Page : www.duranno.com
Address : 95 Seobinggo-dong, Yongsan-gu, Seoul, Republic of Korea

Originally Published in Korean under the title:
하나님의 대사1 (which means 'Ambassador of God')

First English edition was published by Kyujang Publishing Company in April 2012

All Scripture quotations, unless otherwise indicated, are taken from the Holy Bible, New International Version.

ISBN 978-89-531-1988-8 03230

Ambassador of God

1 A Man of the Holy Spirit

Kim Ha-Joong

DURANNO

CONTENTS

AMBASSADOR of GOD

Foreword.

Almost four years have passed since the Korean version of 《Ambassador of God 1》 was published on January 25, 2010. Amazing things have happened during this time. The book has sold over 350,000 copies and was awarded "The Most Popular Christian Book Award" in 2010 by a Christian daily newspaper in Korea. The Korean Christian Publication Association (KCPA) and Korean Christian Booksellers Association (KCBA) selected the book as the number one best seller loved by Korean Christians in 2011. Furthermore, the Cooperation Committee for Mission through Writing, the most respected coalition of different Christian Associations such as KCPA and KCBA, honored me with the 'Author of the Year Award' in 2011.

This all was possible only by the grace of God. Every time I met non-Korean pastors or missionaries, I was asked to translate the book into English. I also received similar requests from Korean missionaries. When an American intercessor prayed for me in 2009, she prayed that I would be called to write a book that would show the next generation how God is pouring blessings over Korea. This was confirmed when I visited the U.S. and Canada, as many of the younger second generation Koreans there requested that I translate my book into English.

As I had already been preparing for the English translation of my book, I decided to push ahead with it upon hearing that.

Many people have helped make this book possible. I would like to express my deep gratitude and love to my daughter Sae-Ryo and my niece Connie who have accompanied me through the process. It would not have been possible to publish the English translation without their support. And I am very thankful to Mrs. Na Hyun (Grace) Lee for her wonderful revision of the translation.

As an elder of Onnuri Church, I have decided to publish this English edition through Duranno, which has close ties with the church. I am very much obliged to Pastor Keum Kyung-Yeon who has helped and supported me through the whole process. And I also appreciate all the efforts made by team leader, Ms. Yoo Joo-

Young, and the members of her editing team.

I hope that this English version of the 《Ambassador of God 1》 spreads throughout the whole world. A Japanese version of this book will also soon be published; and various versions in different foreign languages, including Chinese, will also be published in the future.

I pray that those who read these various versions will know that God is alive and will live as prayer warriors of God.

Prologue.

Living a Life As an Ambassador of God

I decided to define my identity in two ways when I was appointed as the Ambassador to China. The first being an Ambassador Extraordinary and Plenipotentiary appointed by the President of the Republic of Korea (South Korea); and the second, an Ambassador of God. I made strenuous efforts to strengthen the relationship between Korea and China during the six and half years I served as the Ambassador. At the same time, I sought and pursued God's will, just as Jesus had prayed, "Your kingdom come, your will be done on earth as it is in heaven." (Matthew 6:10)

I prayed that God's Kingdom would be realized through my work as the Ambassador to China. I performed my duty with a fear of the Lord. I knew that God had entrusted the ambassadorship to me so that I could "declare the praises of him who called [me] out of darkness into his wonderful light." (1 Peter 2:9)

Ambassadors always needed to heed the instructions of their home government and I worked diligently to fulfill my government's orders. As a Christian, I also upheld the instructions of my Commander in Chief of Heaven, God. This book is a record of my prayer journey as an Ambassador of God who sought and obeyed God's will.

As I prayed over the years, I learned that the things that seem impossible to men can be realized, if God intervenes. And this grace is not only for me. It is a privilege God has given to every man and woman who asks and seeks His will. The power of these men and women lie in prayer.

There isn't any prayer that has not been answered when I prayed with the purpose to serve God's Kingdom and His people. I experienced miracles over and over again, when I prayed according to His word. This book is a vivid record of those testimonies.

> But seek first his kingdom and his righteousness, and all these things will be given to you as well. (Matthew 6:33)

Experiencing the Mysterious Ways of the Lord

I went to church on and off until I was in high school because my mother, who was a faithful Christian, wanted me to. I stopped going to church after I entered college in 1965. In the autumn of 1994, I experienced the grace of God and was baptized the following year. My faith deepened when I began to work at the Office of the President in 1998. Beginning in 2001, I started experiencing the great and mysterious ways of the Lord. At that time, I wondered whether I should write about my experiences.

> Let them give thanks to the Lord for his unfailing love and his wonderful deeds for men. (Psalm 107:8)

In the winter of 2003, I asked God while praying, 'Lord, should I publish a book to testify of the experiences I have had in you? I would like to share my experiences with others.'

God gave me peace in my heart about the book. Then in February 2004, I met a pastor who is a prayer warrior. At that time he conveyed a message that he received from the Lord about the book, even though I had not mentioned it to him. The message was that the time will come for me to write the testimony, and the book will reveal God's outpouring of love and blessing for Korea. I understood then that I should write to glorify God, and that the Lord chose me to write because of His love for Korea.

This pastor's message also confirmed what I had prayed in the winter of 2003. Following this encounter, the responsibility laid heavy on my heart, but it was not easy to spare the time to write. It was only in February 2009, after I was resigned as the Minister of Unification, that I began to work on the book.

Waiting for the Lord's Response

Then there was a long period of time, when every attempt to write the book would not flow. I realized then that the Lord was not allowing me to write, so I stopped trying. Instead I read the Bible and diligently attended revival services and bible studies. In the meantime, on October 4, 2009, I had an opportunity to meet an intercessor from the United States at a small gathering.

She was visiting Korea to lead a revival service. After dinner, the host requested the intercessor to pray for those who were present. She agreed. When it was my turn, she prayed that the time had arrived for me to write the book, to testify about how God had led and guided me so far. She added that if I did not record the testimonies in a book, the next generation would not have the opportunity to know about God's outpouring of blessing over Korea.

These prayers reaffirmed the words that I had received during prayer. It also aligned with the message from the pastor I mentioned above. I had not shared that I was planning to write a book and yet the intercessor declared it in front of almost 20 people. From that moment on, I began to prepare to write the book.

In my time of waiting, God blessed me with opportunities to work on so many things. He also gave me the revelation that having me wait was so that the time would be ripe to publish this book.

This book is a record of only a fraction of what I have experienced in the Lord. It was difficult to select the episodes as there are so many others. If God allows, I plan to continue to publish more books to testify of His works.

In 2001, I heard that the amount of intercessory prayers for me was like the amount of water falling over Niagara Falls. I firmly believe that a few more of these big falls of intercessory prayers were added while I served as an Ambassador of God.

Some people who read this book might think, "How could this be? It must be either strange coincidences or completely fabricated." However, I know that my Lord will keep me safe from such criticism. Such conviction comes from the fact that this book was written in accordance with His plan and intervention. The Lord also had me prepare for the book for a long time. I wrote this book based on the records of all my prayers that I had kept on a daily basis for many years. Many others can also bear witness to my story.

The Calling to Be an Ambassador of God

After His resurrection, our Lord Jesus Christ, who has all authority in Heaven and on earth, sent every one of us as Ambassadors of the Lord to all nations.

> All authority in heaven and on earth has been given to me. Therefore go and make disciples of all nations, baptizing them in the name of the Father and of the Son and of the Holy Spirit, and teaching them to obey everything I have commanded you. And surely I am with you always, to the very end of the age. (Matthew 28:18-20)

We, who are Christians, are Ambassadors of God. God has sent us as Ambassadors to companies, schools, governments and various other fields. Esther, in the Old Testament, understood that the reason she became the queen of Persia was to save her people.

> And who knows but that you have come to your royal position for such a time as this? (Esther 4:14)

Similarly, Nehemiah, who was a beloved subject of King Artaxerxes of Persia, used his position to serve the Israelites who had returned to Jerusalem from captivity. Likewise, it is the duty of every Ambassador of God to work for the Kingdom of Heaven and its people.

It is only through prayer that our duty can be accomplished effectively. However, we should not pray according to the flesh, in which we talk to God without listening. We should pray in the Spirit and only then are we able to communicate with God.

> And pray in the Spirit on all occasions with all kinds of prayers and requests. With this in mind, be alert and always keep on praying for all the saints. (Ephesians 6:18)

I write this book in part to show that praying in the Spirit, as written in Ephesians, will realize God's Kingdom on this earth and will improve the spiritual welfare of God's people.

Ambassadors of God do not pray for their own selfish ambitions. I have always tried to pray for God's Kingdom and righteousness, rather than for my own benefit or for my family's success. In that sense, this book is like my own Book of Acts. This book attempts to illustrate how God led me to serve His beloved people and how He responded to my prayers through the power of the Holy Spirit.

This book shows how the Lord has worked in my daily life. I pray that God will work in similar ways in your lives. I believe that many who read this book will believe in the Living God, learn to pray in the Spirit, and seek guidance and counsel from the Lord. If you pray in the Spirit, you need not worry or be anxious; you will be able to forgive and love others, becoming a person of the Holy Spirit, learning to lead a courageous life in God.

If readers are summoned to become Ambassadors of God, who will serve God's people, the book will have served its purpose. I pray that Ambassadors of God, who pray in the Spirit, will rise up everywhere.

On the morning of my 63rd birthday,
January 9, 2010
Kim Ha-Joong

Chapter 1

Embarking on a Journey of Faith

I started crying as I was listening to the prayer. As the prayer continued, my crying turned into weeping. The tears flowed down my face and I began to choke on the mucus that rose from my throat; it was the first time in my life I had ever cried like that.

Youngest Son Born to a Mother of Faith

My mother was born into an aristocratic family in the beginning of the 20th century. She was the only child in the family. My grandmother, who was a widow, became a Christian and my mother accepted Jesus as her Savior along with my grandmother. But when my mother married my father, who was from a non-Christian family, she could not go to church on Sundays or practice her Christian faith.

Soon after the Korean War broke out in 1950, my father's business failed and our family struggled from financial difficulties. Our financial situation was very dire and my mother had no one to turn to. In her desperation, my mother went back to church and she sought God; she began to wholeheartedly rely on Him.

I was born the youngest of six children. My mother gave birth to me when she was forty-two years old. My mother was always more lenient and loving towards me. This may have been because I was the youngest. No doubt she loved my brothers and sisters, but she was always more forgiving when it came to me. My mother never scolded me. My brothers and sisters complained that this was not fair.

From the time when I was in college, my mother would kneel outside of my bedroom door at dawn every day and she would pray for hours. I sometimes could not go to the bathroom because she was praying right outside my room and I did not want to disturb her.

When my mother said grace for a meal, she prayed for every single person in the family. By the time she finished saying grace, the meal would often be cold.

My mother did not have much material possessions, but she always shared whatever she had with those who were less fortunate. She often stressed the importance of loving and sharing with others.

“Love others. Be gracious and give to others.”

Her teaching left a deep impression on me. I always gave whatever little I had to my friends or colleagues who needed help. It did not matter if I gave them all I had. I gave whatever I had and many people mistakenly thought that I came from a rich family. In the early years of our marriage, my wife and I always quarreled because of my habit of giving money to others. As a civil servant, I did not earn much, and I knew my wife struggled with this, but if there was someone in need, I had to help them first and deal with the consequences later.

This compassion that I felt for others was something I had inherited from my mother.

No More Stepping Foot Into a Church

I went to church occasionally until I was in high school. Our family was poor when I was young so I attended church during Easter or Christmas because I enjoyed the tasty crackers they passed out to the children. Another reason I went was because church was one of those rare places where I could meet girls freely even though I was too shy to even talk to them. I did not read the Bible but because I liked music I memorized many hymns. However, I stopped going to church after I entered college.

I passed the Foreign Service Exam in 1973 and started working in the Ministry of Foreign Affairs. I married my wife Bae Young-Min the year after. Young-Min's family was Buddhist. I told my mother that Young-Min was not a Christian and asked if that would be okay with her. My mother answered, "Do not worry about that. Marry her if you love her." My mother seemed to have a plan.

We lived close to my older brother's place, where my mother lived, after getting married. On Sundays, my mother came to our house, and took my wife to church while she let me sleep in. My wife went involuntarily; since she grew up in a Buddhist family, my wife was frustrated that she had to go to church and complained to me every Sunday.

"Why does your mother take me to church? I'm not a believer; you are! But how come she leaves you alone?"

Every time my wife complained, I asked my wife to be understanding of my mother and to do as she asked. After all, my wife only had to go to church once a week.

My brother at the time owned a two-story building, which he leased commercially. He allowed a small church to occupy the second floor for eight years, and my mother practically lived there. Despite all her efforts, though, I refused to go to church.

In the spring of 1976, I was posted to the Korean Consulate General in New York. My wife and I went to a Korean church once or twice. We felt smothered by the attention we were getting from the members of the congregation and stopped going to church altogether. When we completed our service in New York, we returned to Seoul and then went on to serve at the Korean Embassy in New Delhi, India. We lived in New Delhi for three and half years and returned to Seoul. We still did not go to church.

Touched By God

In October 1986, I went to Beijing on an official mission. From Beijing, I called my wife after dinner and she sounded excited.

"I went to church this evening!"

I was astonished and asked her, "How come? Why did you go to church?"

"My close friend asked me to go with her."

"Oh, really?"

"I think I met the Lord today."

"What? What do you mean?"

My wife told me that she experienced God during the service. I thought that it was an isolated incident and that it was an illusion she had met God. When I returned from the week-long mission I noticed that my wife was a completely different person. All she talked about was God and how she wanted to meet Him again.

'What in the world happened to her?' I asked myself.

I was puzzled by the change in my wife, but at the same time, I did not really mind it either. From then on, I drove my wife and children to church on Sundays. I would drop them off, come home to do some work, and go back to pick them up. Sometimes I would attend the Sunday service with my wife.

When my mother heard about this, she was very happy. My mother had been praying for my wife for many years. My mother knew that God had answered her prayers; she knew that God had touched my wife's heart.

After accepting the Lord, it was my wife who took my mother's place of praying for me. For the next eight years, my wife prayed that I would accept the Lord, just as she did.

My Daughter's Fasting

I was posted to our Embassy in Tokyo towards the end of 1988, and three years later I was sent to serve at the Korea Trade Representative Office in Beijing. My wife, determined to gear up her prayers, and also asked many other people to pray for me. I knew she was doing this but acted as if I did not know what was going on. I thought that if I acknowledged her efforts, she would try to persuade me to go to church.

In the autumn of 1994, my daughter who was in her second year at Beijing University said that she had something to discuss with me. I rarely had time to sit with my daughter and talk because I was always too busy with work. So, when my daughter approached me that day, I became curious and wanted to hear what she had to say.

After sitting down, I asked my daughter, "What is it that you want to talk about?"

My daughter looked at me and said, "Dad, it's time you accepted Jesus as your Savior and started going to church."

I was surprised. I assumed that maybe she wanted to talk about someone she liked or about her career path, or maybe she wanted me to buy her something. When I heard her asking me to accept Jesus Christ as my Savior, I did not know what to say. I responded unenthusiastically.

"Why?"

My daughter looked at me solemnly and said, "I will fast until you start going to church."

I simply told her, "Sure, go ahead."

I thought she was joking. But for the next several weeks, every time she returned from her dormitory on the weekends, she did not eat from Friday evening to Sunday evening. She would sit in front of me during meal times and not eat.

I asked her, "Why aren't you eating?"

She replied, "I told you I'm fasting until you go to church. But don't mind me; please go ahead and eat."

This continued for about three weeks and I thought to myself, why should I not go to church if that is what my daughter so desperately desires?

Finally, I relented and told her that I would go to church and asked her to stop fasting.

Soon afterwards, there was a special revival service at the Beijing 21st Century Korean Church, where my wife and children attended. Since I had promised my daughter that I would go to church, I decided to go to this revival service. Although I had planned to go only once, something remarkable happened to me during the service. I felt so peaceful listening to the praise songs. The speaker's words also moved my heart.

I thought to myself, 'I am a real sinner, but God gives me so many blessings even to a sinner like me. I am so thankful!'

It dawned upon me then that I needed to believe in God. At the same time, fear came upon me.

'If I want to succeed in this world, I need to drink at times and even lie at times for my own benefit. If I become a Christian, does that mean that I will not be able to lead such a life anymore? If I believe in God, I can't continue to live the life of a sinner. But how will I make my dreams come true if I can't do those things?'

In spite of these questions, my heart was telling me that I needed to go back to church.

My Mother's Bible

It was December 11, 1994. I was on a business trip to Luoyang City, Henan Province, China. I was in the middle of dinner with the local Chinese officials when I received a call from my older brother in Seoul.

"Mother lost consciousness. Even if you hurry back right now, I don't know if you will be able to see her before she passes away."

There was no airport in Luoyang at that time so I took a taxi early in the morning to a neighboring city. I, then, flew to Beijing and caught a flight to Seoul. When I arrived at the hospital, my mother was not conscious but was still breathing. My siblings told me that she must have been waiting for me and told me to talk to her. I spoke into my mother's ears.

"Mother, Ha-Joong is here."

At that moment my mother started moving her lips as if she wanted to say something. I started massaging her cold hands and feet and said, "Mother, I'm here. Don't worry about anything." Tears flowed down from my mother's eyes. My mother passed away a few hours later.

My mother, who had prayed every morning for me since I was a little boy, passed away when I was just beginning to take those fateful steps towards God. Even when I was not attending church, my mother used to tell me, "I know that when you receive Jesus as your Savior, you will believe in Him with all your might. I, therefore, have no worries about you."

I remembered those words when we buried her. I cried again when my siblings and I went through her possessions and came across her Bible and hymnal. I told my siblings that I did not need any of her other belongings and only wanted her Bible and hymnal. The Bible was tattered and she had underlined many parts in red. She also had a bookmark on which she had written:

"Thank you, Lord God. I want to do your will and not my own. Amen!"

"Follow Daniel's footsteps and his faith."

"Submit to God and be at peace with him; in this way prosperity will come to you." (Job 22:21)

On the plane back to Beijing, I promised myself that I would now accept Jesus as my true Savior and that I would live the life of faith that my mother so wanted. To this day, I carry the Bible and the hymnal wherever I go as a reminder of my mother's deep love for me.

The First Extraordinary Experience

In 1994, my wife and children were members of the Beijing 21st Century Korean Church. The church had about three hundred members in the congregation at the time and was fairly large for a Korean church in Beijing. Here, my wife met many people who truly loved God. One of them was Deacon Lee Kwang-Ja (currently an evangelist at the Beijing 21st Century Church). She is what we call a "prayer warrior," and she was also one of the strongest supporters of the church. Deacon Lee had fasted for forty days on a number of occasions. Although she was petite, she had a strong grip that you could not pull away from if she were holding onto your hands; but more importantly, she was a strong person spiritually.

In June 1994, the Ministry of Foreign Affairs confidentially informed me that I had been informally designated as the next Director-General for the Asia and Pacific Affairs Bureau. The Ministry added that they wanted me back in Seoul by the end of August. I was still not a believer yet. During that time, Deacon Lee was mentoring my wife, and one day Deacon Lee asked her if she had any specific prayer requests. My wife told her that we wanted to return to Seoul soon.

"We have been overseas for five and half years. Our eldest son will be finishing his junior year in high school and if we do not get transferred to Seoul this time around, we think it might be best if we at least take him back to Seoul (so that he can enroll in a university in Korea)."

Sometime after that, Deacon Lee told my wife that the Lord had shown her that we will only return to Seoul in January of the following year and would not return in August as we had planned. When my wife told me what Deacon Lee had said, I did not quite know what to make of it. It had already been formally decided that I would be appointed to the post of the Director-General. The Ministry of Foreign Affairs usually announces the personnel changes in December and the actual move happens towards the end of February. There was no precedence of staff moving in January. My wife knew the situation well so she did not believe it either.

However, about 10 days later, I heard from Seoul that it would be difficult for them to transfer me back to Korea that fall. Headquarters wanted me to return only at the end of the year. During the extra four months I stayed in Beijing, many things happened. My daughter fasted for me, and I returned to church after thirty years; and my beloved mother had passed away. And that December, we had a new Minister of Foreign Affairs, making my plans to return to Seoul unclear. Just as Deacon Lee had prayed, in January of 1995, the Ministry of Foreign Affairs suddenly announced that I was appointed as the new Director-General for the Asia-Pacific Affairs Bureau, and instructed me to report back to Seoul by mid-January. I was the only person in the entire Ministry who returned to headquarters at that time of the year.

Everything happened just as Deacon Lee foretold. I was amazed that what she had heard from God about me really happened. Not only did she tell us that we would not return in August, but she also knew the exact timing of our return.

It was quite extraordinary and I realized that God spoke to people like Deacon Lee and let them know about His plans ahead of time.

This was the first supernatural experience I had after I became a believer.

Baptized

My wife wanted me to be baptized before our return to Korea. I had been going to church only for a few months. I did not feel ready and told her so. My wife was stubborn. She told me that if I was too busy, the pastor of our church and a few of the church members were willing to come and hold the baptism service at our home. I could not refuse any longer.

So on January 9, just three days before my departure to Seoul, I was baptized with water in our own home. My 47th birthday was also on the same day. Around six o'clock in the evening, Pastor Park Tae-Yun and a few of the deacons came to our home. As soon as Pastor Park poured water on my head, tears rolled down my face and I felt something warm come into my body. I lost my senses for a few seconds and I opened my eyes a little while later.

'Where am I? Why am I kneeling down?'

When I looked down, I realized that I was staring at the carpet in our home. 'This is our home. . . There is my wife and people from church. Yes, I was just baptized. . .'

Everyone was looking at me because I was so still. Pastor Park also looked slightly flustered as it was not customary for people to react like this when being baptized. It felt like a few seconds to me, but in reality, many minutes had passed by. It was the first time I experienced the presence of God.

'This must be what it means to be baptized by the Holy Spirit! Now, I really must live like a child of God!'

Experiencing the presence of the Holy Spirit during my baptism was only the beginning. God had amazing plans in store for me.

Prayer and Alcohol

After we came back to Seoul, I started attending Onnuri Church. For a while, I cried every day. I cried when I walked, I cried when I ate, and I cried when I knelt down to pray. Every time I thought of all the sins I committed, I felt so ashamed in the presence of the Lord that I could not help but cry. I had lived the life of a prodigal son. I got drunk, gossiped and criticized people, and lied. I cried during worship services and I cried during the Holy Communion. I could not help but cry when I thought about Jesus who had died on the cross for my sins. My wife got so used to my crying that she carried a couple of handkerchiefs in her bag.

During this time of repentance and grace, the social pressure to drink alcohol weighed heavily on my heart. When I was in India, I could not drink simply because the weather was too hot. When I came back to Seoul and began socializing with my friends, I started to drink again. During the six years I worked in Japan and China, I drank but did not drink excessively as was the custom in those countries; however, being in Korea was completely different. When I came back to Seoul from Beijing, alcohol was waiting for me.

I disliked the fact that in Korea, the majority of the time, people went drinking for a second round after finishing dinner. Normally, people went to karaoke bars to sing and drink more alcohol. As a way to prevent excessive drinking and discourage people from wanting to go for a second round of drinks, I started circulating the "bomb shot (also known as the boilermaker)," a potent mixture of hard liquor and beer that inebriated people quicker. I would make these shots immediately after sitting down to have dinner and offer it to people at a rapid pace; pretty soon people would become so intoxicated that they would usually forgo the second round. It was a useful way to prevent the night from becoming endless and I could go home early.

Once I came home, I would exercise for an hour to get rid of the alcohol in my body in order to prevent any hangovers. But after a few days, I would have to drink again. Repeatedly, I would make my signature bomb shots and make everyone drink them. Then, I would return home early and exercise for an hour. This went on for weeks and months.

Considering how important drinking is considered in Korean culture and how difficult it is to avoid it, I asked God for help. My prayer was answered when I became the Special Assistant to the Foreign Minister in 1997. The Foreign Minister was known to dislike drinking and he disapproved when others drank. So, I had a great excuse to stop drinking without offending anyone. And in February 1998, I was appointed as the Chief of Protocol to the President which again was the perfect excuse to stop drinking. Being the President's Chief of Protocol left me no time for any other activities, let alone drinking, but more than that, I was given the perfect reason to stop drinking altogether.

Defection of Hwang Jang-Yeop

In February 1997, I had just been appointed as the Special Assistant to then Foreign Minister Yoo Jong-Ha. Hwang Jang-Yeop (now deceased), the former President of North Korea's Kim Il-Sung University and the Secretary of the Labor Party, had entered the Consular Office of the Korean Embassy in Beijing on February 12 to seek asylum. In the emergency meeting that afternoon, the Korean government decided to dispatch me to China to negotiate with the Chinese authorities. The defection of Hwang, who was considered the "private tutor" of Kim Il-Sung and the highest-ranking member of North Korea (ranked 20th in the North Korean power hierarchy), was considered shocking; everything had to be conducted discreetly and efficiently.

Before heading to Beijing the next morning, I asked many people to intercede for me. It was a daunting responsibility and I knew it was not going to be easy to bring Hwang safely back to South Korea.

The day after I arrived in Beijing, Moon Bong-Ju, the Minister for Political Affairs at the Korean Embassy in Beijing (currently a pastor at Osaka Onnuri Church), and I started negotiating with the Chinese authorities. During the daytime, I negotiated with the Chinese officials and also met with my Chinese friends. In the evening, I came back to my hotel and knelt down to pray. On February 19, the former Paramount Leader of the People's Republic of China, Deng Xiaoping, passed away. My superiors back in Seoul instructed me to secretly return to Seoul between February 22-25.

Once back in Seoul, I immediately debriefed the Minister of Foreign Affairs, the Head of the Korean Central Intelligence Agency (KCIA) and the Senior Secretary to the President for Foreign Policy and National Security on the progress made thus far. After I finished my briefing, they asked me for an estimate as to when this case would be resolved. I answered, "It will take four to six weeks."

I was confident that this issue would be resolved within that period of time because I had already prayed about it when I was in Beijing.

My answer startled them. "Are you sure that it will only take four to six weeks?"

They doubted my judgment and questioned whether it would be possible to successfully negotiate with the Chinese authorities within that short period of time. Then, they stressed that I did not need to hurry.

"Exercise caution as this is a matter of great importance." they told me.

"If you can really resolve the matter within that period of time, you will have served the country well." they added.

I replied, "I will do my best so that it can be resolved within four to six weeks."

On February 25, I returned to Beijing to continue the negotiations. The Korean reporters were on the look-out for me as they wanted to learn if there was any progress with the negotiations. Therefore, I disguised myself by dressing like an ordinary Chinese man, riding in a Chinese car that was driven by a Chinese driver. I wanted to make sure that I was not spotted by the reporters or anyone else who was interested in our negotiations.

Moon Bong-Ju and I made certain that we maintained ultimate secrecy and restarted negotiations with the government of China. The negotiations were difficult but it proceeded on schedule and the Chinese government allowed Hwang Jang-Yeop to leave for the Philippines on March 18. 35 days had passed since Hwang stepped into the Consular Office of the Korean Embassy in Beijing, and approximately four weeks had passed since I had talked to the senior officials of the Korean government.

The Power of Intercessory Prayer

The day after Hwang Jang-Yeop left for the Philippines, I had dinner with Tang Jiaxuan, Vice Minister in the Chinese Foreign Ministry. Soon after I arrived in Seoul, I went straight from the airport to the Blue House (Office of the President) and debriefed the members of the Security Coordination Meeting. Participants at the coordination meeting warmly congratulated me on a job well-done.

I had completed this mission in 35 days. When I returned to the office, there were many letters from my colleagues on my desk. Most of the letters said that they were praying that the Hwang Jang-Yeop matter would be resolved smoothly. Within the pile of letters, I came across one written by a young clerk that cleaned my office.

"Since the day you left, I prayed to God every day that your mission would be successful. Please accept my heart felt congratulations."

I was deeply moved by the letter. I realized then that I was able to successfully tackle the challenge in such a short period of time because many people had been praying for me. God had listened to their prayers and helped me.

After I resigned as the Minister of Unification in February 2009, I was invited to speak on the subject of prayer at a church. After the service, I was approached by one of the government officials who had been involved in this mission. He said to me and others, "I always wondered how Minister Kim was so sure that he would be able to solve the case within four to six weeks. And even though I witnessed how quickly the Hwang Jang-Yeop case had been resolved, I kept wondering how this could be possible. Only today was I able to understand why. I had no idea Minister Kim prayed so much."

Historically and politically, the Hwang Jang-Yeop case had a lasting impact on the relations between South Korea and China, and between China and North Korea. Personally, the case taught me how powerful intercessory prayers are.

Blue House (The Office of the President)

In December 1997, Kim Dae-Jung was elected president. Not long after the election, Foreign Minister Yoo Jong-Ha wanted to talk to me.

"The transitional committee of the President-elect asked the Ministry to submit a list of potential candidates for the Chief of Protocol to the President (the Ministry of Foreign Affairs has its own Chief of Protocol but the President's office also has a Chief of Protocol who works directly for the President). I was wondering if you wanted your name to be included in this list. What do you think?"

I replied, "Thank you, Mr. Minister, but more than serving at the Office of the President, I would prefer to go overseas as an Ambassador."

The Foreign Ministry, therefore, submitted a list of three candidates to the Transitional Committee without my name on it. Soon afterwards, the Committee announced the name of the person who was designated as the Chief of Protocol to the President. Then, I was told that the designated person did not go to the Transitional Committee to start his appointment, which I thought was strange.

On February 20, a few days before the inauguration ceremony of President Kim Dae-Jung, I received a message that the Transitional Committee was looking for me, and was told that the Chief of Staff-designate Kim Joong-Kwon wanted to see me. I went over to the Transitional Committee office to meet him.

The Chief of Staff-designate told me, "You have been chosen to be the new Chief of Protocol, so please come into the office on February 23 to begin your work."

Even though I initially was not interested in the post, for reasons beyond my control, I started working as the new Chief of Protocol to the President. When I reported for work on February 23, I had only one full day to prepare for the inauguration, which was scheduled to take place on February 25. On the day of the inauguration, I went to President-elect Kim Dae-Jung's private residence in Ilsan (north of Seoul) at seven o'clock in the morning and officially started my work as the Chief of Protocol to the President.

Not long after I started working in the Blue House, I began to experience something strange. One day, I took a guest to the President's office and I suddenly had inklings that this person might be imprisoned later. I told Director-General Hah Tae-Yoon (later Ambassador to Iraq), who was with me at the time, that I thought this person might go to prison in the near future. Some time had passed and I had the same feeling when I escorted in another guest, and again, I shared this with Director-General Hah. Director-General Hah did not understand why I kept telling him that these people would be imprisoned, but surprisingly enough, those very people ended up going to prison.

One day, however, I had a dream that I was going to prison. I was so shaken by the dream that I woke up immediately. I knelt down and started to pray, but I could not shake off the uneasiness I felt in my heart. So, I woke my wife and asked her to go to the early morning prayer service with me. I had never been to an early morning service before, but ever since that day, until I left the Blue

House, I went to church to attend the early morning prayer service every day.

I usually left home around 5:30 a.m. and went to the six o'clock service. I then left church around 6:50 a.m. for the office. Although I spent around 50 minutes at church, there was not much time to pray as there was praise and worship before the sermon. In total, I only had 15-20 minutes to pray. So I continued to pray in the car on my way to the office.

'Lord, I am going into work now. Please give me wisdom and power to handle the work you have entrusted me with today.'

I prayed for all my engagements and important meetings and also prayed for the people I was going to meet that day. I prayed to God whenever I had time, no matter where I was and no matter what I did.

Forgetting to Pray

As the Chief of Protocol, I went into the President's personal office numerous times a day for two specific reasons. One, was to usher in guests, and the second, was to brief the President on his daily itinerary, as well as different pending issues, and have him review and sign important documents.

I always prayed before I went into the President's office to brief him. I would usually request the President's personal secretary for time to brief the President. When the President's personal secretary would call me over the interphone to come in, I closed my eyes and prayed after hanging up the phone. It did not matter where I was; I always prayed. Sometimes, I prayed as I was at my desk, or other times, I prayed as I was sitting on the sofa. Only after I finished praying would I go in to brief the President. Once I was already standing in front of the President and remembered that I had forgotten to pray before coming in. I was trying to figure out what to do and remembered Nehemiah in the Old Testament who looked up to the sky and prayed to the Lord.

I told the President.

"Mr. President! I'm sorry. I forgot something. I will be right back."

President Kim looked up and said, "Sure, please go get it."

After stepping out of the President's office, I looked for an empty room, and prayed in the room.

'Lord, I am going in to brief the President now. Please give me courage and wisdom.'

Because I prayed, I was always prepared to honestly answer any of the President's questions without fear. From time to time, I would forget to pray and would ask the President to be excused. One day, President Kim smiled and asked, "Secretary Kim, what do you keep forgetting?"

"Mr. President, I apologize."

I would say no more but I think the President somehow knew that what I forgot was not something bad. He would have been upset if I kept forgetting important documents. I do not think he knew that it was prayer that I forgot, but he must have felt something spiritually as he never really got upset with me. The Blue House was a training ground for me where I started to prepare for all things by praying to God first in any circumstance.

The King said to me, "What is it you want?" Then I prayed to the God of heaven. (Nehemiah 2:4)

I See Everything

Between attending early morning prayer services and praying on my own, I wondered whether God was listening to every single one of my prayers. 'Does God listen to all my prayers at the early morning prayer service, the prayers I pray in the car, the prayers at my desk, the prayers on the sofa, or the prayers I prayed when I make the President wait for me? Does He really listen to me?'

In January 2001, my wife told me that my daughter's friend Kim Ji-Yeon, a missionary, was coming to our house. She suggested that I meet Ms. Kim and receive prayer from her. I usually went to the office after Sunday service, but that day I waited for Ms. Kim at our home, and when she came, I asked her to pray for me.

"Can you pray for me?" I asked.

"Yes, let's do that." She answered.

Ms. Kim, my wife and I got ready to pray together. Ms. Kim asked my wife to get some tissues. When my wife came back with a box of tissues that had been opened, Ms. Kim asked for a brand new box of tissues. My wife came back with a new box. Ms. Kim then took out all of the tissues and spread it out on the floor. I was surprised and asked Ms. Kim, "Why are you putting the tissues all over the floor?" She simply answered, "You will know in a little while." After putting the tissues all over the floor, Ms. Kim said, "All right then, let's pray."

As soon as she started praying, she started speaking amazing words.

"My son! I know how much you love me. I have seen you pray. I have seen you pray at the early morning prayer service. I have seen you pray when you are in the car, and I have seen you pray when you are standing in front of your desk. I have seen you pray when you were sitting on the sofa. I have also seen you go into an empty room to pray to me. My son, I truly love you."

I started crying as I was listening to the prayer. As the prayer continued, my crying turned into weeping. The tears flowed down my face and I began to choke on the mucus that rose from my throat; it was the first time in my life I had ever cried like that.

What was more amazing was that Ms. Kim was also crying just like I was, and she also kept spitting something out on the tissue. By the time she ended the prayer, we had used up the entire tissue box. I was at a loss for words. I thought to myself, 'I didn't tell Ms. Kim how I prayed. It was my secret.'

I realized for the first time that God listens to all of my prayers. 'God truly sees everything! It is true!' After this, no matter what people said, I was confident that God listened to my prayers.

> But God has surely listened and heard my voice in prayer. (Psalm 66:19)

Speaking the Language of Heaven Over the Phone

On January 21, 2001, the annual Ambassador's Meeting convened in Seoul. I had lunch with Ambassador Moon Bong-Ju. He was Korea's Ambassador to New Zealand at the time. Ambassador Moon told me about a woman he met in New Zealand named Park Jung-Mi (currently an evangelist living in Washington D.C.).

Ambassador Moon told me that Ms. Park, who was a spouse to a U.S. diplomat, had very special spiritual gifts. He strongly recommended that I speak with Ms. Park over the phone. I had her number but I did not want to call a stranger over the phone, so I asked my wife to call her instead. After the phone call, my wife told me that she had an amazing experience and told me that I should talk to Ms. Park as well.

So I dialed her number and waited. Soon, a lady picked up the phone. I said, "Hello? Is this Deacon Park?"

The lady simply replied, "Yes."

I continued, "Ambassador Moon asked me to call you."

Suddenly, Ms. Park asked me, "Mr. Kim, was there a martyr in your family?"

"No, there wasn't."

She then asked me, "Then, is there a pastor?"

"No, there isn't."

"That is strange then!"

I was wondering what this was all about. I asked, "What is so strange?"

Ms. Park answered, "There is so much intercessory prayer supporting you; it's beyond what our imagination can fathom. I have never met anyone who possessed this much prayer."

I said, "Excuse me? Did you say there is great amount of prayer behind me?"

Ms. Park answered, "It may be difficult for you to understand. I don't know where these prayer came from but there were a tremendous amount of prayers prayed on your behalf."

I told her, "My mother and my eldest sister prayed for me a lot."

"Yes, of course. Even if that were the case, this amount is incredible. Have you been to the Niagara Falls?" she asked me.

"Yes, I have."

Ms. Park went on, "The amount of intercessory prayer for you is like the amount of water falling over Niagara Falls. You don't need to be afraid of anything. Even if people attack you, criticize you or gossip about you, all those words will be swept away by the rushing waters of prayers, like that of the Niagara Falls. There is nothing that you need to worry about."

At that time, I was working at the Blue House, and I was experiencing many things that I considered were spiritual struggles. When I heard Ms. Park say these words, I felt immensely free. Furthermore, Ms. Park seemed to know about the life I had led and what I was thinking at the time. I began to tremble.

Toward the end of our conversation, Ms. Park asked me.

"Mr. Kim, can you speak in tongues?"

"No, I don't know how to."

She exclaimed, "Oh, you must! You can speak in tongues and you need to pray in tongues."

"How do I pray in tongues?" I asked her.

"Let us pray together."

Ms. Park told me to think about Jesus Christ on the cross and repent of my sins. We prayed fervently. Just after a few minutes I started to speak in tongues!

"Mr. Kim, pray in tongues starting today. The gift of tongues is a very important gift from God."

I started to pray in tongues every day. For a while, every time I prayed in tongues I would cough out phlegm. It was as if everything that was diseased and unclean within me were being purged from me. So, I prayed in tongues even harder.

Overcoming Difficulty Through Prayer

When I worked at the Blue House I rarely had enough time to sleep. So when I went to sleep, I never picked up the phone, unless it was the Blue House hotline. My wife knew this; she did not wake me up if I was asleep, even if someone asked for me.

It was a national holiday. I was asleep and the phone at our home started to ring. It was four o'clock in the morning. I, of course, did not pick up the phone and tried to go back to sleep, thinking that whoever was calling would soon give up. However, the phone kept ringing and ringing. It rang multiple times before it stopped. Then, almost immediately, it would start ringing again. The caller seemed determined to continue until I picked up the phone. It did not seem like I had much of a choice. Even though I was angry, I got up and picked up the phone.

"Hello?"

"Mr. Kim, what are you doing?"

It was Deacon Park from New Zealand.

"Deacon Park! It's four o'clock in the morning here. What do you mean what am I doing?" I answered bluntly.

"What are you doing, still sleeping? Something terrible has happened. You must get up!"

I was startled and asked her, "What do you mean?"

"You need to get up now and start praying. Someone will get in touch with you."

Although I was a bit annoyed being startled awake, I became quite alert by the news of something terrible happening. After I hung up, I took a shower and prayed in our living room for an hour. After I prayed, I got dressed and waited for the call.

Around 8:30 in the morning the Blue House hotline phone rang. It was Mr. Shim Yoon-Jo, who was the Secretary for Foreign Affairs (currently a Member of Parliament).

"Mr. Senior Secretary, something has happened. You need to come to the office quickly."

It was quite astonishing. The incident was later reported in the media, but at the time, only a handful people inside the government knew what had happened. It was, therefore, not something that a person living in New Zealand would know. Ms. Park did not know the details of the incident, but while she was praying for me, she had received words from the Holy Spirit and she simply just shared them with me.

Since I had already prayed for an hour, I was relatively at ease when I went into the office. I knew that God let me know in advance so that I could prepare in prayer. I knew He would protect me and guide me. After working non-stop on the incident for a few days, I received a call from Ms. Park.

She teased me, "Mr. Kim, wasn't it tough?"

I answered, "Yes, it was tough."

Ms. Park turned stern and said, "Things have calmed down, but it will continue for a while. Continue praying."

After some time, the incident subsided.

'How can this be?' I wondered to myself. It was the first extraordinary experience I had after receiving the gift of tongues. I came to realize that God is alive and He protects those He loves. God loved me so much that He spoke to Ms. Park, who listened to Him, so that she would pass on the message to me, and I would pray.

Stop Hitting the Wall!

I often knelt down on my bed to pray in tongues. My heart broke when I prayed for my country and my people. When my heart was heavy with the burden of prayer, I sometimes pounded my chest or punched the wall.

'God! Please have mercy on our people!'

One day, Ms. Park called.

"Mr. Kim, do you pray a lot these days?"

"Yes, I do."

"But why do you pray like that?"

I was surprised at her question. "Why? Am I doing something wrong?"

"I shared your name with the intercessory prayer team in Washington D.C. One of the people on the team called and asked me, 'Who is this person? He hits the wall all the time when he prays!' The person who is praying for you also keeps hitting the wall when praying for you. So please stop hitting the wall! Why don't you get a cushion next to you and hit the cushion if you need to."

I was shocked and amazed.

'Someone in Washington D.C. knows that I hit the wall when I pray!'

I again realized that God listens to all my prayers, and that He sees whatever I do. God continued to reveal His presence to me in these many different ways.

> O Lord, you have searched me and you know me. You know when I sit and when I rise; you perceive my thoughts from afar. You discern my going out and my lying down; you are familiar with all my ways. Before a word is on my tongue you know it completely, O Lord. (Psalm 139:1-4)

Committing Fully to the Lord

When I served as the Director-General of the Asia Pacific Bureau at the Foreign Ministry and as the Minister's Special Assistant, my perception of the President was not very different from that of others.

'The President is the most powerful person in the Republic of Korea, so he can do anything he wants to do.'

However, during the three years and eight months I served at the Blue House, I came to realize that even though the President is the most powerful person in the country, there were so many things the President could not do. The public opinion, the opposition party, the media and the civil society, all scrutinized the President's every move. He was not free to do anything on his own.

I thought to myself, 'There are so many things that even the

President cannot do. Then on whom should I rely? Unless God helps me, I cannot accomplish anything that I desire to do. From this day forward, I will only rely on God and trust in Him. If I place half my trust in God and the other half in the world, I will not be able to achieve anything.'

I told myself that I would only trust in God, and I decided to fully commit myself to the Lord. No matter what I did, I was not going to focus on people or depend on them, but rather completely submit all that I do to God. Consequently, as I continued to work in the Blue House, my faith grew deeper.

> No king is saved by the size of his army; no warrior escapes by his great strength. A horse is a vain hope for deliverance; despite all its great strength it cannot save. (Psalm 33:16-17)

A Brother in the Lord

On February 24, 1998, which was a day before I was to begin my official duties as the Chief of Protocol to the President, I received a call from the Administrative Office of the Blue House.

The person from the office told me, "Mr. Secretary, we'll be sending you a car tomorrow morning. Please use the car to go to President-elect Kim Dae-Jung's private residence."

Early the next morning a car arrived at my door.

"Good morning, Mr. Secretary. My name is Jin Geon-Sik and I will be your driver for today."

Mr. Jin was slender but I could tell he had a solid build. Mr. Jin drove me to Ilsan so that I could accompany the President-elect and the First Lady to the Inaugural Ceremony. This is how Mr. Jin and I started my first official day. Later that day, I received a call from the Administrative Office again when I returned to the Blue House after the inauguration.

"Mr. Secretary, Mr. Jin is not your official driver; he was only there temporarily for today. We will ask you to decide on your permanent driver tomorrow."

I told the Administrative Office that I understood. I asked Mr. Jin, "Mr. Jin, until when will you work for me?"

Mr. Jin answered, "I was told only until tomorrow morning. From tomorrow afternoon, there will be a new driver."

The next morning on the way to work, I suddenly had a thought, "Starting this afternoon, I guess I won't be seeing Mr. Jin anymore."

I wondered why God sent Mr. Jin to me on the day of the inauguration of the President. When the car stopped at the Gwanghwamun crossings in downtown Seoul, I asked, "Mr. Jin, would you like to work for me?"

At this, Mr. Jin responded loudly, "Amen!"

"...?"

"I have been praying with my wife for the last six months that I would work for a believer. Thank you so much Mr. Secretary."

As soon as I arrived at the Blue House, I called the Administrative Office.

"I would like Mr. Jin to be my driver."

From that day on, Mr. Jin was my driver during my entire stay at the Blue House.

Soon after I started working at the Blue House, I started going to early morning prayer services. I took a taxi to church and asked Mr. Jin to come pick me up around the time service ended.

One day Mr. Jin asked me, "I would also like to go to the early morning prayer service. May I pick you up at your home so we can go to church together?" I happily agreed. Every morning, Mr. Jin picked me up and we went to church together. Mr. Jin became my brother in the Lord and I started to call him by his name, Geon-Sik. On many of the Sundays, Geon-Sik and I also had lunch together after attending church and before going to the office.

If I did not have scheduled luncheon meetings, I ate lunch with Geon-Sik. As it was not common to see the Chief of Protocol or the Senior Secretary dine with a driver in the drivers' cafeteria, the other drivers would look at me with bewilderment.

Some of them would come up to me and ask, "Mr. Secretary, what are you doing here?"

I would smile and answer, "Well, I came to eat with Geon-Sik."

When Geon-Sik's father-in-law passed away, I spent many hours at the funeral house and people asked me, "Mr. Secretary, why aren't you going home?"

I answered, "Geon-Sik is like my brother. How can I go home?"

I Am Praying that You Do Not Leave

Geon-Sik was also like my guardian angel. Since I served the President I rarely drank, but sometimes I would drink one or two glasses of wine. There was one occasion when I drank wine a few days in a row. On the way to work Geon-Sik asked, "Mr. Secretary! Why are you acting like this these days?"

I was surprised, so I asked him, "What do you mean?"

Geon-Sik looked at me straight in the eyes and said, "Why are you drinking so much wine?"

I sheepishly replied, "Oh, sorry about that."

At another time, Geon-Sik told me.

"Mr. Secretary, you won't be able to leave until the fall of 2001, even if you want to leave the Blue House earlier than that."

"Why not?"

Geon-Sik said, "It's because I am praying that you do not leave."

I was curious. "Why are you praying like that?"

The story was that he had bought a small apartment in Banpo, Seoul, and he was paying the mortgage with his salary and the additional allowance I personally provided him with. Since the construction was going to be completed in the fall of 2001 and the payments had to be made by then, it would be difficult to continue to pay the mortgage if I left. He was, therefore, praying that I would not leave the Blue House before that time.

I was amused. "Ha! So you're praying that your boss does not leave simply because of your mortgage!"

Even though I said that, there was something endearing about what Geon-Sik said.

One day in July 2001, Geon-Sik suddenly said, "Mr. Secretary, you can leave now!" He told me that he had almost completed making payments on his mortgage.

"You really are something!" I shook my head.

But the surprising thing was that I left the Blue House in October 2001. And Geon-Sik moved into the apartment in November of that year. God had listened to Geon-Sik's prayers. Geon-Sik was my partner; he was also God's messenger and a precious brother in Christ.

Chapter 2

Unwavering Faith

One step at a time, God slowly revealed His universe to me, as a parent would teach a child his first words. And when I incessantly prayed seeking His will, He would always meet me with clarity.

My Third Dream

In January 1995, I was appointed as the Director-General for Asia and Pacific Affairs at the Ministry of Foreign Affairs. I had to transfer to Seoul promptly after the appointment was announced. On my last Sunday in Beijing, I attended the worship service at the Beijing 21st Century Korean Church. When it was time for announcements, Pastor Park Tae-Yun shared with the congregation that I would be returning to Korea soon.

"Minister Kim Ha-Joong has completed his services in Beijing and is returning to Korea. I would like to invite him to share a few words with us." I had not expected Pastor Park to invite me to speak. As I walked towards the stage, I started to wonder what I should say, but once I stood in front of the congregation, words began to flow from my mouth as if I had prepared a speech. Now that I think back upon the situation, I realize that it was the Holy Spirit speaking through me.

"I had three dreams when I was young. The first one was to become a diplomat, and the second was to take part in the negotiations to establish diplomatic relations between Korea and China. As you can see, God granted me both of these wishes. I now have one last dream, which is to become Korea's Ambassador to China. God has fulfilled my first two dreams and I believe that He will also help me realize my last." I finished by saying, "I will return to Beijing, within ten years, as Korea's Ambassador to China. I hope to see you again at that time."

It occurred to me, when I returned to my seat, that what I said was a little outrageous. The people in the congregation were probably thinking the same thing. 'How ridiculous! Who does he think he is pretentiously saying that he will return as the Ambassador to China within ten years?'

Praying to Prepare for the Future – Ten Years Later

I was praying one day after I had returned to Seoul, and a thought came to my mind.

'When I left Beijing, I announced to the entire congregation that I would return as the Ambassador within ten years. What am I doing now to prepare for that?'

But strangely, the more I prayed about it, the more confident I became that I would one day be appointed as the Ambassador. I, therefore, changed my prayers.

'Lord, I believe that you will make me the Ambassador to China within ten years. I know that you will fulfill my third dream just as you have done with my first two. Lord, thank you for giving me the opportunity to serve as the Ambassador to China!'

I started to pray prayers of thanksgiving as if I were already the Ambassador to China; and then I continued to pray year after year.

'Lord, when I become the Ambassador to China, I do not want to be an average Ambassador. I want to be an Ambassador who contributes to the strengthening of the relationship between Korea and China. I want to be an honorable Ambassador who will go down in history. Lord, identify the future Ministers, Deputy Ministers, and people who will wield great influence in Chinese society in ten years time. I will pray for them for the next ten years. If I pray for these people for ten years, would they not be of great help to me? Lord, please let me know who these people are.'

And then I listed all the Chinese people I met during the three years I served in China and started asking God about them, one by one.

'Lord, is this the person?'

God gave me wisdom as I prayed, and He let me know in my heart who to include on my list. I was able to come up with a list of approximately twenty people. I made a resolution that I would pray for these people for the next ten years.

I had prayed for six years and ten months by the time I was appointed as the Ambassador to China. By then, the list had expanded to include around forty people. I had met many Chinese friends during the seven years I was working in Korea, and I included their names when God impressed them upon me.

I took the list with me to Beijing in October 2001, and when I returned to Korea as the Minister of Unification in March 2008, the list had expanded to approximately eighty people. From the day I created the list, I prayed for these people every day and I continue to pray for them. I have prayed for some people twice a day for 19 years, which brings the total number of prayers I prayed for each person to be over 10,000.

Appointed As the Ambassador to China

When I was working at the Blue House, I read many books on China. Sometimes, I would read these books in the car. I wanted to be fully prepared when I became the Ambassador to China. One day Geon-Sik said, "Mr. Secretary! You will go to Beijing as the Ambassador to China."

"Ambassador to China? How can I become the Ambassador to China?"

I had never spoken to Geon-Sik about China so I was surprised.

"Well, you read books and articles about China all the time, so you will go to China as the Ambassador!"

Geon-Sik knew what I was thinking. And as Geon-Sik had predicted, I was appointed as the Ambassador to China soon afterwards.

Towards the end of August 2001, the Grand National Party (which was then the opposing party, but now the ruling party) tabled the legislation to dismiss the Minister of Unification Lim Dong-Won. The Grand National Party questioned some of the activities the South Korean non-governmental delegation engaged in while they were visiting Pyongyang to coordinate the commemoration of the August 15 Independence Day with North Korea. I was serving as the Senior Secretary for Foreign Policy and Security and I had close working relations with Minister Lim. I was concerned about what would happen if the legislation passed. To my dismay, on September 3, the National Assembly passed the bill. After Minister Lim was dismissed, I became worried because the post of Minister of Unification was too important to leave vacant for very long.

Four days later, after attending the early morning service, Geon-Sik handed me the morning paper and exclaimed, "Mr. Secretary! You are going to be the next Ambassador to China!"

I looked at him and said, "What do you mean?" I took the newspaper from Geon-Sik and started reading.

The newspaper headline read, 'Ambassador to China Hong Soon-Young as the Minister of Unification, Senior Secretary for Foreign Policy and Security, Kim Ha-Joong as the new Ambassador to China.' A few days later, I was officially appointed as the Ambassador to China.

I arrived in China as the new Korean Ambassador on October 8, 2001. It was just as I had dreamt and prayed for. On the first Sunday I was in Beijing, I attended Sunday service at the Beijing 21st Century Korean Church. Pastor Park Tae-Yoon was at the door and warmly welcomed me. "I knew you would be back as the Ambassador!" Pastor Park beamed at me.

"How did you know?" I asked.

Pastor Park explained, "Remember what you said when you were leaving Beijing? I was moved when I heard you say that you were coming back as the Ambassador within ten years. From that day onwards, I prayed that you would indeed return as the Ambassador. And then some time later, I realized that unless the President sent you here that you would not be able to come to Beijing, so I started praying for the President as well."

I learned that many of those who were in the congregation that day prayed daily that I would return as the Ambassador. I understood then that it was the Holy Spirit that led me to publicly announce that I would return as the Ambassador. Those who heard me say this or those who heard this story had prayed for me all these years.

If you believe, you will receive whatever you ask for in prayer. (Matthew 21:22)

Overcoming Trials Through Intercessory Prayer

On October 7, the day before my departure to Beijing, I received a call from Ms. Park Jung-Mi in New Zealand.

"Ambassador, I heard that you are leaving for China tomorrow."

"Yes, I am."

"You need to pray a lot." She told me.

"Why do you say that?"

"There are forces of darkness attempting to bring trouble upon you. You need to be cautious, but most importantly, pray a lot." She solemnly warned me.

I assured her, "Yes, I will."

"You really need to pray a lot." She insisted again.

"Yes, I understand."

But soon after I arrived in China, I was so busy attending to official business - submitting my credentials to the Chinese President and going on rounds of courtesy calls to the diplomatic corps and government officials, I only had time to pray for about 30 minutes a day. A week after I started working in Beijing, I attended the Asia Pacific Economic Cooperation (APEC) Summit Meeting which was being held in Shanghai on October 15. I accompanied President Kim Dae-Jung and the Korean delegation to Shanghai. I returned to Beijing after the APEC Summit concluded.

Two days after I returned to Beijing, I went back to Shanghai to celebrate the Korean naval vessels' first-ever entry to Shanghai port. It was there that I received a call from my deputy at the Embassy.

"Mr. Ambassador, a Korean newspaper reported that a Korean drug smuggler was executed in the Heilongjiang Province. We are currently investigating the case. We will take care of this. I think you can return to Beijing as planned."

I returned to Beijing after two days and called a meeting of the senior officials in the Embassy and the Consulate.

We needed to be sure of the facts. "Have we received prior notice from the Chinese government regarding the execution of the drug smuggler?"

"No, we haven't."

I could not understand how the Chinese government could execute a foreigner without informing the relevant Embassy first.

I instructed, "Please look carefully again to see if there have been any communication."

In the early morning of November 2, the Chinese Foreign Ministry announced that they had officially communicated to the Korean Embassy about the execution of the drug smuggler. In response, the Embassy maintained that we had not received any communication. The next afternoon, however, one of the staff at the Consulate found a copy of the fax that had been sent to the Embassy by the Chinese government, informing us of the pending execution. Once this was made known, public opinion in Korea towards the Korean Embassy and the Ministry of Foreign Affairs and Trade deteriorated rapidly. The media continued to criticize the Embassy and the government which exacerbated the situation.

It turned out that the incident took place before my arrival; and the fax had been sent to the Embassy at the end of September, also before my arrival, but all of this did not matter. As the Ambassador, I was the one with the responsibility to resolve the issue. I also had to make sure that this issue would not strain Korea-China relations.

Amidst all of this, I remembered what Deacon Park told me before I left Seoul. She had told me to be diligent in prayer but I had not done so because I was too busy. I knelt down and immediately repented before God.

Ms. Park called from New Zealand not long after.

"Ambassador, you had a rough time, didn't you?"

"Yes, it was rough." I admitted.

"That is why I told you to pray diligently."

Ms. Park was the spouse of a U.S. diplomat working in New Zealand so she did not know much about Korea's current affairs. Yet, because she prayed and listened to God, she could convey what the Holy Spirit desired for me to know before my arrival in Beijing. The Lord truly works in amazing ways.

Prayers Led By the Holy Spirit

In the spring of 2002, a mid-level official in the Korean Foreign Ministry came to see me at the Embassy. He was in China on an official mission and requested a meeting with me.

"Mr. Ambassador, I pledged to do a special 40 days of early morning prayer back in June 2001. On one of the mornings when I was praying at church, the Holy Spirit moved my heart to pray for you (Note: at that time I was still the Senior Secretary to the President). Because I did not know you, I had no plans to pray for you. I, therefore, stopped praying and told God that I did not know you well. The Holy Spirit, however, urged me to continue to pray for you. I had many other things to pray for but I continued to pray for you. And then you left for China as the Ambassador."

He continued, "In October last year, I saw the media reports about the execution of the drug smuggler. I understood then why the Holy Spirit urged me to pray for you. I was planning to continue to pray for you the next day at the early morning service but for some reason no words of prayer came. I think it was because I had filled that bowl of prayer by then. It was the first time I had such an experience so I wanted to tell you in person."

I was touched by his story. God already knew that difficult times awaited me and warned me through Deacon Park. At the same time, He had someone who did not know me that well pray for me. I came to realize how deep His love is for me and committed my life to Him again.

I started interceding for this official from that day onwards. Whenever he faced difficulties, I listened to God on his behalf and he was greatly encouraged by God's words. He is now in an Ambassadorial position.

Ask Me Everything

After arriving in China as the Ambassador, I realized that there were many difficult problems to solve. China is a vast country with 1.3 billion people. Since I was the highest ranking official representing our government in China, many people came to seek my opinion. I received instructions from our headquarters on a daily basis but there was no one I could turn to for help. I needed to be responsible and accountable for everything. I prayed diligently every day but it was difficult to discern where His will was.

In December 2001, Ms. Kim Ji-Yeon came to Beijing.

She prayed for me. "Be sensitive to my words. Ask Me. Ask Me everything before making any decision, however small it may seem. I will answer all of your prayers. Do not move a step before you ask Me. Do not ask Me only about important things, but ask Me about the small things too. Then, I will teach you and show you My will."

I could not believe this at first. But I started writing out all of my prayer requests on a piece of paper and prayed according to that list. I was curious whether God was really going to communicate His answers to all of my prayers.

Eight months passed by. I was praying like any other day and all of a sudden I could not breathe. My facial muscles twitched and my tongue kept going in and out of my mouth. There was nothing I could do to control it. It was the first time my wife or I had experienced anything like it. We asked a couple of pastors, that we knew, but they did not seem to know why this was happening either.

I was alarmed and asked my wife.

"Do you think maybe I've been possessed by an evil spirit?"

My wife was not sure so she sat next to me when I prayed. Every time this happened, she would pray to God asking Him to take away the evil spirit but the phenomenon just continued. At the same time, I could not stop praying just because my body was acting in a strange way, so I continued to pray.

One day, I was praying when the same thing happened. I became breathless and felt like I was suffocating. My facial muscles twitched again and my tongue hung out. Then, I fell to my side. I could not breathe; and as I was gasping for air, suddenly a thought crossed my mind.

'Oh, this isn't me! It must be the condition of the person I am praying for!'

The more I thought about it, it became clearer to me. My body was behaving differently according to the person for whom I was praying. Sometimes I felt I was breathless, sometimes I felt like I was being strangled, sometimes my facial muscles twitched and sometimes my tongue stuck out.

I understood then that this was the language the Holy Spirit was using to communicate with me. The Holy Spirit had been trying to communicate with me all along but since I could not comprehend Him, the Holy Spirit was using my body to help me descern its meaning.

After this realization, I was able to understand that my physical manifestations and its intensity, reflected the spiritual state of the person I was interceding for. I met and called people to confirm my discernment. Then, a few months later, my manifestations began to include weeping and wailing as well.

Communicating with the Holy Spirit

The year passed by and in January 2003, I was praying to God about a request I had.

'Dear Lord, this is really important for our country, so please help me.'

While I was praying, my arms suddenly went up and I started to sing a praise song in tongues. I did not know the tune of this song.

'What is this song?' I wondered.

I continued singing for a few minutes. When I finished singing, my arms came down as well. It was a strange experience. I then started praying about another request. This time my arms did not go up. I moved to another prayer request, and this time, my arms went up and I began to sing in tongues again. It was a different song this time. I realized that there were two different songs. I differentiated the prayers according to the two songs. I marked the prayers where I sang the first song as 'Praise A', and the second as 'Praise B' and waited to see what happened with these prayer requests.

Later, I found out the meaning of this strange phenomenon. The prayers that were prayed when my arms went up, were fulfilled, but those that I prayed when my arms stayed down, were not. Furthermore, the prayer requests to which I had sung 'Praise A' were accomplished in an extraordinary manner, while the prayer requests with 'Praise B' were answered but in an ordinary way. I realized that because I did not understand what the Holy Spirit was saying to me, the Holy Spirit was lifting up my arms and giving me songs to help me distinguish the answers.

One time when I was praying, my arms did not go up. My wife who was watching me told me to lift my arms up, and when I tried, it felt like someone was pushing my shoulders down with a heavy piece of metal. My arms did not budge. Unless the Holy Spirit lifted my arms, they would not move. I found this remarkable, and it made praying fun. I looked forward to my times of prayer and was full of joy that the Holy Spirit was communicating with me.

Every day I compiled all the prayer requests I had into a list. I listed the names of people I was going to meet and the important issues I had to tackle that day. If my arms were lifted, I would mark 'O', and if they stayed down, I marked it 'X'. The Lord had indeed started to communicate His will to me as He had promised through Ms. Kim. I gave a prayer of thanksgiving, and also repented that I had doubts about God's promise.

Hearing Clear Messages

The Holy Spirit lifted my arms for over a year. Once, when I prayed for an hour, my arms would go up about ten times within the hour. My arms were in the air for about 30 to 40 minutes. It was difficult having my arms up for that long every time I prayed, so I asked God if He could change His means of communication.

'Lord, it is too tiring to continue praying like this. My arms hurt and I have many more things to pray for. It also seems to take a lot of time. Would you teach me a simpler way of communication?'

After that prayer, my arms stopped going up. I was worried that God was not speaking to me anymore. I even regretted that I had asked Him for a different way of communication.

But in a little while, the Holy Spirit started to speak to me in my heart strongly with 'Yes', 'No', 'Do it', or 'Don't do it.' I realized that the Holy Spirit had spoken to me before as well, but I did not perceive it because I was not sensitive to His voice. However, I had become more attuned to the voice of the Holy Spirit as I prayed for the last year and a half, and was now able to understand the Lord's will. I knew very clearly that the Holy Spirit was talking to my heart, although it was not as obvious as my arms being lifted up.

One step at a time, God slowly revealed His universe to me, as a parent would teach a child his first words. And when I incessantly prayed seeking His will, He would always meet me with clarity.

It was similar to when David asked God whether he should go to war and God answered.

> So David inquired of God: "Shall I go and attack the Philistines? Will you hand them over to me?" The Lord answered him, "Go, I will hand them over to you." (1 Chronicles 14:10)

> In the course of time, David inquired of the Lord. "Shall I go up to one of the towns of Judah?" he asked. The Lord said, "Go up." David asked, "Where shall I go?" "To Hebron," the Lord answered. (2 Samuel 2:1)

I wholeheartedly believed the words He gave me and began to obey His commands. Faith began to take its root deeper within me.

Throwing Up Alcohol

In mid-February of 2003, my wife called me at the office.

"I got a call from Korea. Deacon Park Jung-Hee, who is the older sister of Ms. Park Jung-Mi in New Zealand, is coming to

China. They are coming with a tour group and want to stay with us in Beijing after their tour ends."

Immediately, I had a feeling that these people were being sent by God, so I told my wife that we should welcome them into our home.

Park Jung-Hee (currently a pastor) and Lee Jung-Sook came to Beijing a few days later. We prayed after dinner. While she was praying, Park Jung-Hee suddenly said, "Mr. Ambassador, you will soon be able to interpret tongues and also hear God's voice."

I was surprised and said, "Who? Me?"

I could not believe that I would be able to interpret tongues and also be able to hear God's words.

Park Jung-Hee then asked me, "Mr. Ambassador, do you drink?"

"Yes, I do. I usually do not drink, but when there is an official event, I drink a glass of wine or two."

Ms. Park looked at me and said, "Hmm. . . I don't think you will be able to drink wine anymore."

"Why not?" I asked her.

"Because you will begin to throw up alcohol."

"I will?" I said with a smile.

"Yes!" She said excitedly.

"How do you know?" I asked.

"God just showed me a vision where you were throwing up alcohol. There will be a day when you will throw up alcohol and when that happens, you will not be able to drink a drop of alcohol anymore. Afterward, you will go through many amazing transformations."

I was surprised when I heard this and wondered how someone like me, who had regular social engagements as part of his work, would not be able to drink at all.

One month after Park Jung-Hee and her friend left, the way I prayed remained mostly unchanged. My arms went up from time to time when I prayed and sometimes I sang worship songs in tongues. But one day, I was interceding for someone when all of a sudden I started to interpret tongues, 'Oh, Lord. I feel so frustrated. God, please help me!'

Every time I prayed for someone, I would speak out my interpretation of tongues and know exactly what situation the person was in. Now that I knew why the person was facing hardship, my prayers became more specific. This was the gift of interpretation that Park Jung-Hee had told me about. At the same time, I began to hear God's voice in brief moments.

A couple of years later, I continued to drink wine at official events. In December 2005, we were hosting a dinner at the residence for a senior Chinese official. After proposing a toast, I brought the wine glass to my lips, but the glass stopped right before my lips and I could not move my arm, not even an inch. I thought that it might be an early sign of paralysis in my arm. I was stunned and put the wine glass down to massage my right arm. After a while, I picked up the wine glass and tried to drink it again but my right arm would not budge. I, then, leaned forward to bring the wine to my lips, and instantly, I began to throw up. That evening, I could not drink a single drop of wine. I told my wife about this after dinner. My wife was amazed and reminded me of what Park Jung-Hee said.

"Don't you remember? Park Jung-Hee told you a few years ago that you would throw up alcohol!"

"Oh, that's right." I was reminded of what she told me. I went to my study to look at my journal. I found the notes of Park Jung-Hee's prayer on February 26, 2003. I was astonished.

'It is amazing that I, who used to drink ten glasses of so-called 'bomb shots', cannot even drink one drop of wine! The Holy Spirit is truly living in me.' I was sure that the Holy Spirit, who was in me, was pushing out the alcohol.

The Lord Speaking to My Heart

The next evening, I was praying with my doors locked, and I thought I heard someone speak to me. I looked around and there was no one in the room. I restarted to pray, and again, I heard someone speaking to me. I stood up and searched the room. I opened the closet, and even went into the bathroom adjacent to my room and there was no one there. I knelt down to pray again and the same thing happened.

A thought occurred to me that it might be the Holy Spirit speaking to me. I grabbed a pen and paper and started to pray in tongues and wrote down what I heard in my spirit. I read it after I finished praying and realized I had written down things I had not known about the person for whom I was interceding; it included problems at work and with his family and children.

This is how I began receiving God's words. Sometimes I conveyed what I received from the Holy Spirit to the people I prayed for and sometimes I shared it in writing.

The impact this had on people was immense. People who received the written prayers were astounded and some of them would cry. Others were overjoyed to know that God was watching over them. I continued to share God's messages with many people and experienced that God was alive every time. God's words made my faith more steadfast and I became even more courageous in my walk with God.

> In him and through faith in him we may approach God with freedom and confidence. (Ephesians 3:12)

Chapter 3

Victory Through Love and Courage

People who knew me wondered, “How is he so bold? What makes him so courageous?” I was bold because God led me, and all I had to do was follow Him.

War Against SARS

The most challenging time during my years as the Ambassador to China was the outbreak of the Severe Acute Respiratory Syndrome (SARS), which was a new infectious disease. SARS first appeared in Guangdong, China, in November 2002, and then rapidly spread to thirty different countries. By the time the World Health Organization (WHO) announced that SARS was under control, approximately 8,500 people had been infected by the virus and 800 people had died.

What concerned WHO at the time was that the SARS virus was highly contagious. There was no vaccine or drug available to prevent or cure the infection and it was very difficult to detect it in its early stages. SARS spread swiftly around the world as the virus was transmitted to other countries via aircraft and other modes of travel. In order to contain the spread of infection, WHO advised against all but essential travel to the Guangdong Province, Hong Kong, Beijing, Shanxi Province in China and Toronto, Canada. This was one of the strongest advisories issued by WHO in recent years and was later expanded to include the Huabei area in China.

The sense of anxiety heightened and unfounded rumors spread throughout China. Schools were closed and the Chinese government restricted travel. Despite these efforts, people who lived in the high risk regions moved back to their hometowns, and accordingly, SARS spread to different parts of China at a rapid pace. The Chinese government prescribed its efforts to stop the transmission of the virus as a "war" against SARS.

Many countries followed WHO's advisory and recommended against their citizens traveling to China. Furthermore, some countries even limited issuing visas to Chinese nationals. At the same time, foreigners who were living in China, whether they were working or studying, returned to their home countries. Many international events were either canceled or postponed, and foreign dignitaries canceled their visits to China. The economic activities in the country almost came to a full stop and the government was not able to function normally.

Corporations from the U.S., Japan and other industrialized countries decided to evacuate their employees from China as the situation worsened. On April 3, 2003, the U.S. Department of State issued an "Authorized Departure" notice and evacuated all of their non-essential staff and families of the U.S. Embassy and Consulate Generals in China and Hong Kong on a voluntary basis.

Koreans who resided in China also became very anxious. The

Korean Embassy in Beijing established a SARS Task Force. It closely liaised with the Korean community, corporations, and students in China and deliberated on ways to protect the lives of Koreans residing in the country.

However, as it became more difficult to foresee when the Chinese government was going to bring SARS under control, both the SARS Task Force and the overseas Korean community thought that evacuation was inevitable. It was time for me to decide whether we would evacuate. Korean expatriates who had home offices or headquarters in Korea especially wanted the Korean Embassy to issue the evacuation order, as this would enable the branch offices to officially request their headquarters for monetary support. I had, therefore, been praying and asking for wisdom.

In mid-April, I prayed to God.

'Lord, I will issue an evacuation order like the other governments.'

'Do not evacuate.' I was told.

I prayed again.

'Lord, Koreans in China are worried about the situation here and are waiting for the Embassy to issue an evacuation order.'

God assured me, 'I will not let any of your people in China be infected by the SARS virus. Do not leave this country.'

I was relieved to hear in my heart that God would protect all the Koreans in China and that not a single Korean would be infected by SARS. My heart became more and more bold as I continued to pray.

> So do not fear, for I am with you; do not be dismayed, for I am your God. I will strengthen you and help you; I will uphold you with my righteous right hand. (Isaiah 41:10)

The Tears of the Premier in a Vision

After God spoke to my heart that I should not order the evacuation, I still had some doubts and wondered whether I had correctly heard God's voice. A few days later, I saw a vision when I was praying. (I rarely see visions and even till this day, have only seen a few.) A gentleman who was wearing a tie was weeping. I could not see his face but I knew he was Chinese.

A few days later, I was watching the news and Chinese Premier Wen Jiabao came on television. He said, "I weep these days when I think of the Chinese people who have been suffering from SARS." At that moment, I knew the gentleman I saw in my vision was Premier Wen Jiabao. I realized that God was giving me a confirmation that the decision not to evacuate the Koreans was a correct one.

I continued to see Premier Wen in the news. When SARS was

at its peak, Premier Wen went to the affected areas to provide support to the people who lived there. In a meeting with Beijing University students, Premier Wen was in tears as he shared that he could not sleep at night because he was so worried about SARS.

He added, "We do not blame the heavens nor do we blame man. We consider this as a challenge to our country. I was encouraged when I saw our flag at the welcoming ceremony for the French Prime Minister. I was reminded that while China has gone through many difficult times during the last few thousand years, our country has never faltered. The more obstacles we faced, the more bold we became. I believe that the Chinese people will overcome this crisis, united and stronger."

As I listened to Premier Wen's words, I was confident that China would be able to eradicate the SARS virus very soon.

Koreans Will Not Be Infected By the SARS Virus

I called a staff meeting after God showed me the vision. My staff briefed me about the preparations they had made to issue the evacuation order. One of the staff members updated me on the current situation and the details of the charter flight schedules.

I stopped him and asked, "What are you talking about?"

Everyone looked at me and became quiet. It was clear my staff did not understand why I was asking this question.

"Who issued the evacuation order? The evacuation order can only be issued by the Ambassador. I did not issue this order. May I ask who decided for me?" I looked around the room.

The staff had awkward expressions on their faces.

"People can leave if they want to, but I will not issue a mandatory evacuation order under any circumstance."

One of the senior officials at the Embassy spoke up, "What do you mean, Ambassador? Our people, the corporations and the students, they are all concerned."

I looked at him and said, "SARS may spread all over China but not a single Korean will be infected by the virus. I will take on all responsibility as the Ambassador. If we leave China when the Chinese are going through one of their most difficult times, how are we going to return to this country and expect to have a good relationship? We need to stay here and provide support to the Chinese. They will sincerely appreciate our gesture and it will further strengthen the relationship between our two countries."

Nonetheless, my staff consistently insisted "Mr. Ambassador, please approve this order."

But I was firm, as God had given me confirmation.

I continued, "The relationship between Korea and China is very special. Korea and China are geographically very close. If we evacuate our nationals, our decision will also have an impact on other governments' decisions. If we evacuate, people from countries that are geographically far away will feel threatened as well. Our actions will only highlight the danger China is in. We do not need to further trouble China during this time of trial. We need to support their efforts to eradicate SARS. I believe in the Chinese government's ability to control SARS. We need to share the burden with the Chinese. A friend that stands by when things get difficult is a real friend. We need to turn these challenging times into an important turning point in our relations with China." I ended the meeting with these words.

After the meeting, a few senior officials in the Embassy, including Minister Cho Hwan-Bok (later Ambassador to Mexico), who was in charge of economic and SARS related affairs, came into my office.

"Mr. Ambassador, we understand how much you love China. However, the situation is very serious. What will you do if Koreans become infected with the SARS virus?"

I said to them, "That will not happen. If that happens, I will assume all responsibility."

We organized another staff meeting a few days later. I stressed to the staff again the reasons why we were not going to evacuate the Koreans, the confidence I had in the Chinese government, and the importance of Korea-China relations. I also explained how our actions would impact bilateral relations and asked for their understanding and support. This time, I could feel that their attitudes had slightly changed. I sensed that God was moving their hearts.

Touching China's Heart

We proceeded to act quickly. The Embassy staff raised $3,900. The spouses of the staff also raised $1,000, and in total, we donated $4,900 to Beijing City's Hygiene Department. The Chinese media widely broadcasted our donation, as our action stood out when people of other nations were leaving China. Many Chinese people were touched when our actions were reported by the news.

China's new government had just been formed in March of that year and SARS was the first crisis this government had to face. I recommended to my government that the President and Prime Minister of Korea send a message of consolation to the Chinese government. I requested that the Korean government provide a donation to the Chinese government as well. The Ministry of Foreign Affairs acted on these recommendations.

Korean President Roh Moo-Hyun called Chinese President Hu Jintao and conveyed his message of support. The Korean Prime Minister Koh Gun also sent a message of consolation to the Chinese Premier Wen Jiabao. The Korean government pledged a contribution of $100,000, which was symbolic of our support to the

Chinese government. When we informed the Chinese government about this gift, we were told that the Minister of Civil Affairs would receive it himself. I visited the Chinese Ministry of Civil Affairs on the morning of April 30 to hand deliver the contribution.

The grateful Minister said, "On behalf of my government, I would like to thank Ambassador Kim for coming to the Ministry of Civil Affairs to personally deliver the Korean government's contribution. This is a difficult time for China, and we would like to publicly share the story of the Korean government's friendship and support with the people of China. We believe this will serve as a new milestone in our friendship."

The Korean corporations that heeded the Embassy's recommendation to stay in China also provided contributions to support the Chinese government's eradication efforts. The Korean community's actions moved the heart of the Chinese government and its people.

After the eradication of SARS, I had an opportunity to meet the President of People's Daily, which is the Communist Party's largest official media outlet with an approximate circulation of 2.3 million. On behalf of the entire Chinese media, the President of People's Daily expressed his deep gratitude to the Korean government and the people of Korea for their support.

"We are grateful to the Korean government, the Korean people and the Korean Embassy's help when SARS broke out in our country. Many of the Western countries had issued evacuation orders but the Korean government showed deep understanding and unfailing support for China. We deeply appreciate the warm gesture."

China noticed that there was no case of SARS in Korea and that not a single Korean national living in China was infected by SARS. Because of this, there apparently was a widespread rumor that Koreans were immune to SARS because of our consumption of kimchi (a Korean traditional spicy pickled cabbage dish). Our Chinese friends were therefore quite happy when we gave them kimchi as gifts. I instructed the Embassy staff to order kimchi from Korea. We then gave it as gifts to hundreds of senior Chinese officials. Many of those officials wrote us thank you letters. We were able to touch China and the Chinese people's hearts during the SARS crisis.

People who knew me wondered, "How is he so bold? What makes him so courageous?" I was bold because God led me, and all I had to do was follow Him.

The scale of SARS was so huge and unprecedented that it was not possible for me to make decisions based on my personal experience or knowledge. Instead, I was able to be bold because God gave me the decision and I simply followed. A person who knows where to go because he understands God's will can always be courageous.

Be strong and take heart, all you who hope in the Lord. (Psalm 31:24)

You Will Meet Him Separately

The Ministry of Foreign Affairs and Trade annually held an Ambassadors Meeting in February. In 2003, President Roh Moo-Hyun had just been inaugurated as the new President, so the Ambassadors Meeting was postponed to May 21-23.

A senior official in the Ministry of Foreign Affairs and Trade called me in the beginning of May when SARS was at its peak.

"There is an official dinner at the Blue House on May 22 hosted by the President. Since you are coming from a SARS affected area we need extra time to quarantine you. Therefore, please come to Korea by May 9, which is two weeks before the Ambassadors Meeting."

This was because there was a risk that people who had been residing in China could transmit SARS. I had already been praying about this matter.

I prayed again that evening and told God that I would return to Seoul at an earlier date so that I can attend the Blue House dinner. However, God told me not to go earlier. So, I called the official at the Ministry.

I told him, "I will return as originally scheduled. There's a lot for me to take care of here at the Embassy."

"Oh, really?"

He was taken aback by my words.

A few days later, the Vice-Minister at the Ministry called me to tell me the same thing. "Mr. Ambassador, you can arrive later if the work at the Embassy is too busy, but I'm afraid you will not be able to attend the Blue House dinner. . ."

I told him I understood the situation and I did not mind if I could not go to the Blue House dinner. I returned home and prayed to the Lord.

'God, I am obeying your words and I will not return at an earlier date, but it is strange that the Ambassador to China won't be meeting the newly inaugurated President. Lord, should I really not return to Korea even a little bit sooner?'

God assured me then, 'You will meet him separately.'

I realized then that God had His plans. So, I started to prepare a briefing note for the President.

When I arrived on May 15, many of my colleagues in the Ministry said, "How can the Ambassador to China go back without meeting the new President?"

I could only smile and answer, "I'm not sure, but there must be a way."

On the day of the dinner at the Blue House, over 120 Ambassadors and their spouses boarded buses at the Shilla Hotel to go to the Blue House. My wife and I ordered room service.

My wife said, "I know you prayed about this but isn't this too extreme?"

I comforted my wife. "Don't worry. We will know what God's will is in a few days."

The next day, I attended the Ambassador's Meeting. Many of the ambassadors felt bad for me, because I could not attend the Blue House dinner. However, I was unmoved. I continued to wait for the Blue House to contact me.

In the afternoon, I got a call from the Blue House.

"Mr. Ambassador, please come to the Blue House on Monday at 11:30 a.m. The President would like you to brief him separately."

I prayed, 'Lord, thank you! You are letting me meet the President.'

I trembled as I was able to experience yet again that God is alive.

Briefing the President

The Protocol Office of the Blue House contacted me again.

"Mr. Ambassador, this is an instruction coming from the top. Since SARS is not contained yet, please do not mention the President visiting China when you brief him."

I told him that I understood. In fact, the government had been reviewing President Roh Moo-Hyun's visit to China soon after his inauguration. We had been discussing a possible visit in early July with the Chinese government but did not make a final decision because of SARS.

That evening, I asked God.

'We were planning to organize the Presidential visit in early July. Since SARS is still widespread, should we postpone it to November?'

God did not answer.

'Shall we then do it in October?'

'. . .'

'Then, how about September?'

Still no answer, '. . .'

'August. . .'

'Then, should we just proceed as planned in early July?'

Finally, God replied, 'Yes.'

I pondered about His answer.

'Why is God telling me to proceed with the Presidential visit in early July as planned?'

I realized that it meant that the transmission of SARS was going to stop by the end of June. If not, we could not proceed with the Presidential visit. I was confident and decided to recommend that the President visit China in early July.

On the morning of Saturday May 24, I went to the Ministry of Foreign Affairs and Trade's Northeast Asia Division. There were only a few staff members working in the office. I worked on the briefing note. In the briefing note, I wrote that SARS would begin to recede in June and recommended that the President visit China in early July as originally planned. I also outlined the expectations of the Chinese government and the anticipated diplomatic accomplishments that would be made through this visit.

I went to the Blue House two days later. The Director-General in the Protocol Office once again reminded me of the instruction from the top and requested that I not mention or talk about the President's visit to China.

I told the Director-General, "It does not matter what the Blue House thinks. As the Ambassador to China, I will recommend to the President that he visit China as planned."

I then went into the President's office with the Senior Secretary for Foreign Policy and the Chief of Protocol. I briefed the President and recommended he visit China in early July.

President Roh Moo-Hyun carefully read over the prepared briefing note and asked me, "How do you know that the SARS crisis will be over by the end of June?"

I answered, "Mr. President, I'm the Ambassador to China and a China specialist. Please believe the Ambassador's words."

The President did not ask me any more questions about SARS.

I wrapped up the briefing and came outside. One of the participants said to me, "Ambassador Kim, you really are something."

He said this because I went ahead and requested that the President visit China in early July, in spite of their request to do otherwise.

I told them, "Don't worry. There won't be any problems."

When I returned to the Ministry, officials were wondering what and how I briefed the President.

"Did you tell the President about his visit to China?"

"Yes."

"What did you tell him?"

"I asked him to come in early July."

"What about SARS?"

"I told you, it will be over by the end of June."

"What if it's not?"

I told them, "It will."

"How do you know? The World Health Organization hasn't said anything yet. What are you going to do if you proceed with the preparations and SARS is not over by the end of June?"

I told them, "Then, as the Ambassador, I must be held accountable, and am willing to take full responsibility."

When I told the senior officials that I was willing to suffer the consequences, they did not dispute me anymore. I returned to Beijing on May 30, after requesting the Ministry to send official instructions to the Embassy, as there was not much time to prepare for the state visit that was to happen in the beginning of July.

SARS Recedes

The Ministry of Foreign Affairs and Trade sent official instructions on June 4. The instruction stated that the President would be in China from July 7 until July 10 for the state visit. I immediately called a senior official at the Chinese Foreign Ministry. The official said that they welcomed President Roh's visit and added that while there were visits of the French Prime Minister in April and the Romanian Prime Minister in mid-May, this was the first state visit by a foreign dignitary since the beginning of the SARS outbreak. The Chinese government promised their full support for the visit.

A Task Force was set up within the Embassy to prepare for the Presidential visit. At the same time, I kneeled and prayed a few times a day. I had spoken with confidence but inside my heart I was worried and nervous.

'Lord, please stop the transmission of SARS by the end of June.'

If the state visit did not happen because the SARS transmission did not cease, I had to be held accountable in one way or another.

I asked my wife to pray as well.

"There is nothing for us to do but pray. If the Presidential visit goes wrong, we will be summoned back to Korea. SARS needs to stop being a threat by the end of June."

My wife and I prayed fervently.

To our surprise, the travel restrictions to the city of Tianjin, Hebei Province, Shanxi Province and the Inner Mongolia district were lifted on June 13. On June 24, the travel restriction to Beijing was also lifted. This was the last travel restriction to be lifted. The Chinese government was able to bring SARS under control.

'Hallelujah! Lord, thank you, thank you very much!'

I deeply thanked God when I heard the news.

On July 5, WHO announced that SARS had globally been brought under control. It was only two days before the Korean President's visit.

President Roh Moo-Hyun's visit proceeded as scheduled. I accompanied the President to the Diaoyutai State Guesthouse from the Beijing Capital Airport. President Roh smiled and asked me to stay for tea.

President Roh said, "I know you said that you are a China specialist but how did you know when SARS was going to end?"

I smiled and answered, "That is why I asked you to believe your Ambassador."

The President let out a hearty laugh.

When the Presidential delegation left for Korea from Shanghai after four days of visitations, I came back to the hotel and knelt down to pray and give thanks to God.

I was grateful for His guidance and for telling me not to evacuate the Koreans after the outbreak of SARS, for not letting me attend the Blue House dinner but letting me meet with the President separately, and for stopping SARS by the end of June so that the Presidential visit could take place.

God, who is so faithful, guided and protected me until the end. He did this for me, so I would not be put to shame, although I had worried that I might have misunderstood His words. He also allowed me to win over the Chinese peoples' hearts through the SARS crisis. I praised God's name and prayed that He would continue to bless China and the Chinese people.

I also prayed that God would bless and comfort the Minister of Economic Affairs Cho Hwan-Bok, and Ms. Jun Eun-Sook from the Korean Food and Drug Administration and other colleagues in the Embassy who worked tirelessly throughout the SARS incident.

> Fear of man will prove to be a snare, but whoever trusts in the Lord is kept safe. (Proverbs 29:25)

God's Plans

In December 2001, which was the year I was assigned to China, my wife returned to Korea to handle personal matters. While she was in Korea, my wife's mentor introduced her to Pastor Lee Kwang-Seop of Jesus for the World Church who prayed for her.

Pastor Lee did not know who my wife was or what I did. He did not have any information about us and yet when he prayed he said, "I see a vision and your husband is standing in the Kim Il-Sung (former leader of North Korea) Plaza." My wife told the Pastor, "Yes, that is correct. My husband has been to North Korea." Pastor Lee said, "No, it is not about the past but it is about the future." My wife wondered if Pastor Lee made a mistake.

"My husband works in China. Perhaps you saw Mao Zedong's portrait in the Tiananmen Square?"

"No, it was Kim Il-Sung's portrait in the Kim Il-Sung Plaza. Your husband will be working on issues related to North Korea. The work is deeply involved with North Korea and it is the starting point of an important work."

When my wife told me this after she returned to Beijing, I kept her words in my heart. A few months after, in March 2002, a group of North Koreans ran into the Spanish Embassy seeking asylum. This signaled a new era of North Koreans running into foreign embassies in Beijing. They also started coming into the Consular Office of the Korean Embassy. During the six and half years I served as the Ambassador to China, I was closely involved in the Six Party Talks and other matters related to North Korea. When I was appointed as the Minister for Unification in March 2008, I remembered Pastor Lee's vision of the Kim Il-Sung Plaza and thought about God's plans.

> Surely the Sovereign Lord does nothing without revealing his plan to his servants the prophets. (Amos 3:7)

The God Who Prepares

I served as the Minister for Political Affairs at the Korean Embassy in China, for three years, starting in February 1992. At the time, the relation between China and North Korea was very close. The North Korean economy was not as bad as it is now; fewer people were escaping North Korea to come to China.

In August 1992, after China and South Korea established diplomatic relations, North Korean asylum seekers came to our Embassy from time to time. However, because of the nature of this politically sensitive situation, it was difficult for us to receive them. Korea-China diplomatic relations had just been established and North Korea's influence in China was still strong. So whenever North Koreans came into our Consular Office or Embassy, we would give them some pocket money and ask them to leave, telling them that there was not much we could do.

In the beginning of the book, I mentioned that after I finished my service in China I returned to the Ministry of Foreign Affairs as the Director-General for Asia Pacific Affairs in January 1995. In 1997, when I was working as the Special Assistant to the Minister of Foreign Affairs, I was put in charge of the defection of Hwang Jang-Yeop, one of North Korea's highest ranking officials.

By the time I arrived in Beijing as the Ambassador in October 2001, the North Korean asylum seekers issue became even more sensitive and complicated. On March 14, 2002, 25 North Korean asylum seekers dramatically ran into the Spanish Embassy in Beijing, generating global interest. We contacted the Spanish Embassy, and they worked closely with the Chinese government. In the end, the Chinese government decided to send all 25 of the asylum seekers to South Korea via the Philippines.

However, in May 2002, five North Korean asylum seekers tried to enter the Japanese Consulate in Shenyang, but three of them failed and were caught by the Chinese police. The two family members who were successful in entering the Consulate were also taken in by the Chinese police. These five were the relatives of the 'Kilsu's family' who had sought asylum at the Beijing office of the UN High Commissioner for Refugee in June 2001.

Soon afterwards, the North Koreans sought asylum in the U.S. Consulate in Shenyang and the Canadian Embassy in Beijing. Every time this happened, we worked with the embassies and sent all of these asylum seekers to South Korea. I started to worry about what might happen in the near future. I realized that these people would soon seek asylum in the Korean Embassy and I thought about what we should do.

If the North Korean asylum seekers came into the Korean Embassy, we would have to directly negotiate with the Chinese government. Since South and North Korea are still at confrontation, and because China has close relations with North Korea, it was a complicated issue. Many diplomats at the Embassy were worried about the impact it would have on our relationship with China, if we accepted the North Korean asylum seekers.

However, as the North Korean asylum seekers had already entered the embassies or consulates of other countries, it was difficult for the Korean Embassy to refuse them. I prayed to God about this and every time I prayed, God gave me courage and strength. I guarded my heart and prepared for the day when North Korean asylum seekers would enter the Consular Office of the Korean Embassy.

Rescuing 1,000 People

As expected, the North Korean asylum seekers began to come into the Consular Office, which was in a different location from the Korean Embassy starting in May 2002. The negotiations with the Chinese government were as difficult as I had imagined. I asked God for help. I also prayed to God that He would bless the Chinese government for working on a difficult issue, and prayed for the Chinese people who were responsible, so that they would have compassion in their hearts.

Some of my staff were not pleased that the Embassy was accepting the asylum seekers. So at every meeting, I spoke about why we should accept them.

"It is rare for people to have the opportunity to save the lives of others, no matter how rich or powerful we are. This is why I am grateful that I have been given the opportunity to save the lives of others. While I remain Ambassador to China, I will accept North Korean asylum seekers under any circumstance and will delightfully endure all difficulties. Even though we are not able to rescue the asylum seekers that are on the streets, we will negotiate with the Chinese government to ensure that those who are with us in our Embassy are sent safely to South Korea. I want to save as many people as possible. I have prayed that I would be able to rescue 1,000 North Korean asylum seekers during my service here. Please join me in this endeavor."

When I mentioned how I hoped to rescue a thousand lives, I was referring to the 'Schindler's List'. Oskar Schindler, who was a businessman during the Second World War, is remembered for saving over 1,000 Jews during the Holocaust. I wanted to help save as many North Korean asylum seekers.

Of course, the North Korean asylum seekers issue could not be compared to Schindler's List, the Chinese government was very cooperative on this matter. However, because of the political situation, this issue did place China in a difficult position and I was sympathetic to the discomfort the Chinese government was experiencing.

By the end of September, the number of asylum seekers we were hosting had reached 112. The maximum number of asylum seekers that the Consulate could host was about 50-60 people and our capacity had been exceeded. It became difficult for the Consular Office to function properly. At the same time, it was difficult to expect the Chinese government to provide swift cooperation.

Closing Down the Consular Office

I came to the realization that it would be best to temporarily close down the Consular Office. I conferred with the senior officials in the Embassy. Many of the officials reacted negatively as they were not sure how the Chinese government would respond. Headquarters informed us that it was up to the Embassy to make the final call.

Therefore, I had a decision to make. I prayed and prayed. God continued to tell me to be strong and courageous; and He reassured me that it was okay to close down the Consular Office. So, I did. On September 29, 2003, we sent a Note Verbale to the Chinese Foreign Ministry and sought their understanding.

"The Consular Office of the Korean Embassy has surpassed its maximum capacity by hosting a large number of North Korean asylum seekers. We have no alternative but to temporarily close our Consular Office."

I simultaneously met with Chinese officials from the Foreign Ministry and explained our situation. I informed them that the Consular Office would be closed down temporarily from October 7, onwards.

We also announced to the public that the Consular Office would temporarily close and explained the reasoning to our Korean correspondents as well. The Korean media widely reported that the Consular Office of the Korean Embassy stopped providing civil services with headlines such as "Korean Consulate Stops Business."

Headquarters was worried about the implications the closure

might have on diplomatic relations. I conveyed to headquarters that the Embassy had reviewed all factors before making the decision. I continued to pray.

'Lord, do not let this become a diplomatic issue and please resolve this matter smoothly. Please move the hearts of the Chinese government leaders and all those who are responsible for this matter.'

Soon after the Consular Office closed, the Chinese government contacted the Embassy and inquired how many North Korean asylum seekers needed to be sent to South Korea in order to reopen the Consular Office.

Hallelujah! I thanked God for His help.

The Chinese government allowed 29 of the 112 asylum seekers to leave the country and the Consular Office reopened, providing civil services just two weeks after closure. Other foreign embassies were astonished that we had decided to close down the Consular Office on the basis that the Chinese government did not provide clearance for the asylum seekers to leave the country. They were surprised because they knew that closing down the Consular Office took a lot of courage. I was able to close the Consular Office not because we trusted our diplomatic skills but because God had given me courage. God also moved the hearts of the Chinese government leaders and bureaucrats.

The Emergency Squad

The negotiations with the Chinese government were difficult and the consulate staff also suffered. They had to work under difficult conditions as over one hundred North Korean asylum seekers were living inside the Consular Office.

The staff had to work in the corridors in order to provide living space for the North Koreans. They had to provide food and clothing as well. And because people were not allowed to go outside, they became easily irritated and overly sensitive. There were all kinds of incidents, all the time. When SARS was rampaging throughout the country, the staff was worried that the asylum seekers would get infected.

Despite these conditions, the Consul General and the staff did their best to help them. I always went in to the office on holidays and weekends, except when I was away for business. I wanted to be available if something happened at the Consular Office and take immediate action if necessary; the Consul-General, the consulate staff and I were like the emergency squad.

The staff members who did not understand the seriousness of the asylum seekers situation thought it was strange that the Ambassador went in to the office almost 365 days of the year. There were rumors that the Ambassador was "torturing" his staff by going into the office every day, but I did not explain myself or respond to such rumors, because I knew how sensitive the issue was.

Before leaving to assume the duty as the Minister for Unification in 2008, I received an update from the Consular Office regarding the situation of the North Korean asylum seekers. During my years in Beijing, the asylum seekers had entered the Consular Office over 410 times between May 2002 and February 2008, and the number of North Koreans sent to South Korea had exceeded 1,000. I was surprised when I saw this number. God had indeed answered my prayer! I was able to help rescue a thousand lives.

The fact that we had solved over 410 incidents meant that we had contacted and negotiated with the Chinese government a few thousand times. It was only possible because God had helped and moved the Chinese officials' hearts.

After I saw the numbers, I knelt down to pray and give thanks to the Lord. I asked God to bless those Chinese officials who had helped many North Korean asylum seekers go to South Korea via a third country.

Furthermore, I prayed that God would bless the colleagues in the Consular Office ,who worked 24/7, to ensure that nothing went wrong. I want to especially recognize Consul-General Mr. Lee Jun-Kyu (currently Ambassador to India), Consul-General Mr. Yu Ju-Yul, Consul-General Mr. Lee Kyung-Su (currently Deputy Minister for Political Affairs, MOFA), and Consul-General Mr. Jun Tae-Dong (currently Consul General to Istanbul).

A Strange Dream

It was January 2003. My wife had returned to Korea for my father-in-law's memorial and had an opportunity to meet with Pastor Lee Gwang-Seop once more. Pastor Lee told my wife that he had a strange dream the night before. He had been waiting to meet the person the dream was for and told my wife that it was for her.

The dream went like this. There were two people who were dead and buried. Someone went inside the grave and tapped on these two people. The two people then woke up, and the person who went inside the grave brought out the two people with him.

Pastor Lee added, "I think this dream is about saving two people's lives. I think it's your husband who needs to save their lives. I don't know who these people are but they may be criminals. The reason God is trying to save them is because one of them used to be a believer. But God told me that he is a 'delinquent Christian'."

When my wife shared this story with me, I remembered the two Koreans who had received death sentences in Shandong Province and Liaoning Province in 2002. They had manufactured and smuggled enormous amounts of drugs and had received death sentences. Because 2002 was the year commemorating the tenth anniversary of Korea-China relations, we requested that the Chinese government refrain from executing them that year. The death sentence had been postponed for one year.

I had a feeling the two in Pastor Lee's dream might be these two criminals. I met with the Chinese Foreign Ministry officials and urged them not to proceed with the execution.

I explained to them, "The only time a Korean national was executed outside of Korea was in September 2001. This was when the Chinese government executed our national who had been involved in the manufacturing and smuggling of drugs. The public opinion towards China soured and this has had a negative impact on Korea-China relations. I want to stress that if you go ahead with the execution of these two people, especially when both Korea and China have just formed new governments, the Korea-China relations will deteriorate. I also want to note that Korea has not executed any person whether Korean or foreign national since 1997. Drug dealers are punished in Korea but they are not executed. Please consider this when you make your decision."

The Chinese officials said that they would convey the Korean Embassy's message to the relevant Ministries. I put in a lot of effort to resolve this matter but I was not sure whether these were the same people in Pastor Lee's dream.

A 'Delinquent Christian'

One month later, a Korean parliamentarian visited me.

"There is someone in my constituency who was sentenced to death by the Chinese government because he had been dealing drugs. His wife prays for her husband every morning. The wife came to me daily, crying, and asking me to help her husband. Mr. Ambassador, I would be grateful if you could help her."

The parliamentarian added. "The funny thing is, this person used to be a Christian. I suppose you can say that he is a 'delinquent Christian'."

"A delinquent Christian!"

I realized at that moment that the man in Pastor Lee's dream was indeed the man on death row. I told the parliamentarian about the dream Pastor Lee had and informed him that the Embassy was already negotiating with the Chinese government about his case. I also asked the Parliamentarian to tell the man's wife to continue to pray.

After the parliamentarian left, I thought about what to do next. Since the man on death row was a Christian, I thought it might be better to have a believer work on the case. Counselor Mr. Lee Young-Baik, was that perfect person. Counselor Lee was born in Wuhan, Hubei Province in China, and had attended the overseas Chinese school in Seoul from elementary to high school. He then lived in Taiwan for 18 years. At the time of this case, Counselor Lee had already served 10 years as a diplomat in Beijing. He was South Korea's best Chinese interpreter, and had two years left until his retirement. I asked Counselor Lee to take up the case.

"Mr. Lee, please work on this case. This will be one of your good deeds before retirement. Let's save the lives of these two man. If we pray and work on this case, we will be able to save them. Let's first work to save the man who is on death row in Shandong Province."

I shared the details of the dream and the reason why we needed to save this man. When he finished listening to me, Mr. Lee said, "I understand that you feel sympathetic towards this man. However, in China, people are sentenced to death if they manufacture just 50 grams of drugs. Mr. Ambassador, I looked over the documents. This person alone manufactured 3,600 grams of drugs. He also sold them. It's impossible to save his life."

I urged him to reconsider as I was confident that God would help. "God wants to save his life. Let's give it a try."

Counselor Lee reluctantly replied, "OK, if you say so. I'll try my best."

I, then, contacted the Chinese Foreign Ministry and met with relevant officials to persuade them to change the sentence. I also asked my home government to raise this issue every time there was an important meeting with the Chinese government. Counselor Lee was responsible for visiting the man. After every visit, when Counselor Lee came to brief me, he cried saying that he felt so sorry for the man. I prayed with him and asked God to help us.

In addition to the visits, Counselor Lee also met with many Chinese officials and sought their help.

The Repentance of a Death Row Convict

Our prayers and endless efforts were paying off and our actions influenced the Chinese government's judicial authorities. On August 8, 2003, the Chinese Supreme Court made a ruling stating that due to the Korean Embassy's repeated requests, and in light of humanitarian principles, the death penalty was put on hold. Furthermore, the Supreme Court put the criminals on probation for two years. The criminal in Shandong had received a death sentence in the first court of instance, and in the second court of instance had received confirmation of the verdict. Under normal circumstances, the convict should have been executed immediately but his sentence was miraculously commuted and he was spared from execution. Seven months later, the criminal in Liaoning Province also received a respite.

Counselor Lee reminisced later that he initially did not know how to comfort a convict who was on death row. He did not know what to do or say. He shared his experience in writing:

After much agony and deliberation, I looked through the Bible and found the best way to comfort others. It was "Rejoice with those who rejoice; mourn with those who mourn." (Romans 12:15) Even if I said, "It must be so difficult and challenging to be in here," that was not going to comfort this man.

The first time I visited, the steel doors creaked open and I could hear the shackles clanging against the cement floor. I closed my eyes and started praying. All of a sudden, fear came upon me when I closed my eyes. I felt as if I was falling into an abyss and I had to open my eyes again.

The daylight was so strong that I could not keep my eyes open. When I closed my eyes, fear overcame me again that I could not keep them closed. All of a sudden, I saw that a man, who was 6'2", was standing in front of me. He had handcuffs and shackles around his ankles. We started having a conversation through the steel bars. I asked the ward to undo the handcuffs and the shackles and offered to go inside the steel prison to meet with him.

I had never prayed out loud until that day. I was one of those Sunday Christians who did not seek God's will when I was comfortable and my needs were met. But when I met the criminal, I held his hands and started to pray out loud. Not only that, I embraced the man and began to cry. The Chinese public prosecutor would tease me saying, "Why is the Consul sadder than the prisoner?"

I spoke to the convict about God's love, that there is no one without sin and that God loved us so much, He forgives people like us. I also explained that God is the Supreme Ruler and Majesty. I urged him to repent of his sins and seek God's forgiveness.

"It might be okay for you to die but are you going to leave your wife who is praying for you in tears? And what about your children?"

"Oh, then can I live?"

"Yes, of course!"

"How can I live?"

"Pray, and you will live."

"How do I pray?"

I explained, "Prayer is not about beautiful expressions and well structured sentences. Rely on Jesus Christ and speak to the Lord. Repent of your sins and ask for forgiveness and God who is love will forgive us of our sins."

He listened intently. When I visited him one month later, he said, "It was not easy to pray at first, but now it has become a part of my daily routine. I pray about various things. I feel that my sins have been forgiven." He looked healthier and brighter.

After five months, the sentence was miraculously put on hold for two years, which in reality meant that the death sentence had been reduced to a life sentence. Subsequently, the other convict received the same sentence.

I was ashamed that I had not trusted the Ambassador's faith in the Lord. I tried my best, but all the while not truly believing that I would be able to save these men's lives.

A pastor had a dream and that dream was conveyed to me through my wife. When I was not sure whether the criminals were the men in the dream, God gave me confirmation through a parliamentarian. God used Counselor Lee Young-Baik and the convict repented; both the spirit and the body of this man and the other convict were saved. I was amazed at God's elaborate planning.

> Suppose one of you has a hundred sheep and loses one of them. Does he not leave the ninety-nine in the open country and go after the lost sheep until he finds it? (Luke 15:4)

A Letter from Prison

I received a letter in the winter of 2004. A Korean woman named Lee Young-Hee (pseudonym) sent this letter from a Chinese prison.

She wrote, "I have been praying to God to release me from prison quickly. As I was praying, God gave me assurance that you, who are a believer, would help me leave this prison."

Lee Young-Hee was charged with smuggling Chinese people

out of the country. She had been arrested in June 1998 by the Chinese authorities and received a 12 year sentence in 2001. She was serving her seventh year and she requested to be released on parole, citing different ailments stemming from the long sentence she was serving. Her age was exacerbating her physical condition. According to the Chinese criminal law, a person who has been given a limited penal servitude could request parole once he or she served half of the sentence.

I felt sympathy for this woman who received a sentence that was far more severe than the crime she had committed. I prayed to God and asked for His wisdom.

'Lord, this prisoner is saying that I will be able to help her leave the prison. Can she really leave if I try?'

'Yes.'

I continued to pray and God continued to answer positively.

I first needed to understand the situation of this prisoner. I found out that the prisoner did not have any family or relatives who visited her. The prisoner received necessary supplies and some cash from one of our consuls in the Korean Embassy and had been leading a lonely life in prison. In June 2004, when she had reached the point where she served half of her 12 year sentence, it was reduced by nine months. She then requested that the Embassy help her be released on parole. The Embassy requested the parole but the Chinese authorities had informed the Embassy that this was not possible.

In January 2005, I put together a small team to work on this case. The team consisted of Consul-General Yu Joo-Yul, Legal Attaché Park Hong-Sik (Chief Prosecutor), the Police Attaché and Jun Eun-Sook from the Korea Food and Drug Administration who was given the responsibility of visiting the prisoner. I instructed the team to first hire a lawyer to review the legal aspects, and at the same time, contact the relevant ministry officials to receive support from the Chinese government.

After a few weeks, the task team updated me on the progress.

"Mr. Ambassador, this is impossible."

They mentioned that while the Chinese government released Chinese nationals on parole, the government did not do the same for foreign nationals. This was because it was difficult to monitor foreign nationals, and there were other legal issues involved. The relevant ministries' responses were also lukewarm.

I put the work on hold and continued to kneel down and ask God to intervene. God gave me assurance that I should continue without worrying. Lee Young-Hee sent another letter during this time.

Dear Mr. Ambassador,

Today is a very hot day. I was touched by your colleagues' visit. I feel deep remorse as a Korean national for being in a Chinese prison. I am really thankful for the Embassy staff that visits me, and delivers the food and newspaper to me every month. Please accept my deepest gratitude. My hope is to return to my hometown in Korea. Mr. Ambassador, please stay well and be filled with joy. I will always pray for you.

At the end of her letter, she added a poem that expressed her heart of penitence. She had titled it the "Biblical Poem of Repentance Dedicated to the Ambassador."

Ah! Mine iniquity
Crimson hath been,
Infinite, infinite
Sin upon sin
Sin of not loving Thee,
Sin of not trusting Thee,
Infinite sin.
Then all is peace and light
This soul within;
Thus shall I walk with Thee,
The loved unseen;
Leaning on Thee, my God,
Guided along the road,
Nothing between.
<Excerpt from "No, Not Desparingly" by Horatius Bonar>

God's Way

In June 2005, I put together a second task force. This time we sent diplomatic notes to the Chinese Ministry of Foreign Affairs, the Ministry of Justice and the People's Supreme Court, requesting the early release of the prisoner. The Embassy's Minister for Political Affairs, Consul-General and I continued to be in touch with the Chinese officials and requested her parole, but there was no progress. In October, we sent another round of diplomatic notes and continued to contact the Chinese officials, but there was still no progress.

We tried again in March 2006, and again, but the situation remained the same. During the entire process, I continued to request God's help. God urged me to continue without worrying. I put together a third team and asked my colleagues to continue to work on this matter.

One of the members of the team said, "Mr. Ambassador, we followed your instructions and did our best. We fully understand you are a Christian and that you are doing this because you love and feel compassion for this prisoner, but in reality, this is not possible. I do not think that we should proceed with this matter. I will put my job on the line, if this prisoner ends up being released on early parole."

He meant that he would resign from his job, if the prisoner was released on early parole. I smiled and told him, "Yes, of course. Please be prepared to resign."

Starting that day, I began to pray more fervently.

'Lord, one of my staff members announced in front of many that he would resign if the prisoner is released. I have continued to work on this case because you said that you would intervene. Please do not put me to shame, please help me Lord.'

Just a few days later, in the evening, God spoke to me while I was praying.

'Meet with the Minister of Justice.'

The next day, I requested a meeting with the Chinese Minister of Justice. I thought it would take a few days for the request to be granted but I got a call that afternoon. I was asked to come to the Justice Ministry the next day.

On the afternoon of April 6, I went to the Justice Ministry with the Consul-General, and the Legal Attaché Minister Wu Aiying was waiting for me in the meeting room. The Justice Minister was a tall and elegant lady. She greeted me warmly. Minister Wu told me that she had visited Korea when she was the Deputy Governor of Shandong Province and that she was deeply impressed by Korea.

She added that while she had been serving as the Minister of Justice for over a year, it was her first time meeting a Foreign Ambassador to China. When she heard that I had requested a meeting, she wanted to meet me as soon as possible. Minister Wu asked if I had any requests for her. I shared several issues that were being discussed between Korea and China, and then I raised the issue of parole for Lee Young-Hee. The Minister discussed what I shared with her colleague, who was in the meeting, and said to me, "You have made these requests on behalf of the Korean government and I will not handle it lightly. I will put in my utmost effort to ensure that your request is granted." I knew that Lee Young-Hee would be released when I heard the Minister say this. God had already touched the Minister's heart.

We continued to negotiate with the Ministry of Foreign Affairs and the Ministry of Justice. We were finally informed in June 2006 that the Chinese government decided to grant Lee Young-Hee parole. As the Chinese government needed one to two additional months to complete the process, they had asked us to keep everything confidential for the time being.

Hallelujah! I knelt in front of God that day and cried tears of joy and gratitude.

Right after the Chinese government informed us of their decision, Counselor Park Enna (Director General of Development Cooperation, MOFA) and Second-Secretary Yeo So-Young (currently First Secretary, MOFA) went to visit the prisoner. I told them that they must not inform Lee Young-Hee of her pending release.

The two returned to the Embassy after their visit and came into my office. As they began to debrief me, they started to cry.

"What's wrong?" I asked.

In tears, Counselor Park said, "Ambassador, as soon as we went into the visitor's lounge, Lee Young-Hee said 'I can go out now. I was praying a few days ago and God told me that I would be going out soon. So please continue to negotiate with the Chinese authorities.' We were surprised and did not know what to say. We did not reveal anything to her and just responded, 'We understand that you are going through a difficult time, but if you endure through this time, you will indeed see the light at the end of the tunnel.' We were wondering if any of the wards informed her, so we asked the wards, 'Is there a way for the sentence to be reduced for this prisoner? Have you heard any news from your authorities?' The wards said that there was no word of such a possibility."

Both Counselor Park and Second Secretary Yeo could not stop crying when they were relaying the story to me. I was amazed at how much God loved the prisoner and how He had answered her prayers.

Give Four Times the Amount

Lee Young-Hee's parole was delayed due to the summer holidays. We were finally informed that the Chinese government would release her on parole on November 20, and immediately send her to Korea. I wanted to meet her personally, but I had to go to Xian on a mission the day before. Before I left on the mission though, I prayed for her. While I was praying, I thought that I should give her a small monetary gift since she had been in prison for eight years. I asked God how much I should give her.

'Lord, I will give her some money for her travels.'

God then told me to give her more than what I was planning to give.

'Give more.'

'Then, I will give her twice the amount.'

'You need to give her more.'

'I will give her four times the amount.'

'Alright.'

I did not understand why God wanted me to give her so much money, but I obeyed. Before my departure to Xian, I asked the Consul General and the Police Attaché to deliver the money and the prayer to Lee Young-Hee when they saw her at the airport. They told me later that she cried continuously in front of the boarding gate.

Director-General Jun Eun-Sook who used to visit the prisoner and was now back at the Food and Drug Administration in Korea gave me a call a few days later.

"Mr. Ambassador, I got a call from Ms. Lee. I was so surprised. Even when I was visiting her in prison, I thought that parole would be impossible, but what you said came true. This is a miracle! Just amazing!"

Six months later, Lee Young-Hee who had returned to Korea wrote me a letter.

> "I want to express my deepest gratitude to the Ambassador and the Embassy staff who worked so hard the last two years for my parole. When I returned to Korea, I could not find any family and I did not have a home to go to. I was able to rent a small room with the money the Ambassador gave me, and I continue to live here. Without the Ambassador's help, I would have frozen to death on the streets this winter. Thank you, Mr. Ambassador."

At the end of the letter, she added that she would not commit any more crimes, and that she would continue to pray for me until she died. She also said that she shared with other people about how she was released on parole. I was then able to fully understand why God wanted me to give her four times the amount I had originally planned.

Prayers that Save Lives

The next day, I brought the letter to the staff meeting and asked a colleague to read it out aloud. Then, I said,

"You are diplomats who represent the country. Because you are diplomats, you work hard for the country but you also lead a privileged life. We have been given privileges. This is possible because of the tax our people pay, and we have to serve those people. We need to love and work hard for the Koreans who are leading difficult lives around us. I prayed countless times for a 60 year old female prisoner whom I had never met. From now on, I encourage all of you to help and love other Koreans, who are facing difficulty, more as well."

And I looked at the person who told everyone that he would resign from his job if the prisoner was released.

I looked at him and said, "Why are you still here?"

He stood up and said, "Mr. Ambassador, I'm sorry. I was wrong."

The North Korean asylum seekers, criminals on death row and prisoners, they are all souls who need encouragement and support. God loves these people, and He protected the North Korean asylum seekers, saved the people on death row, and when the 60 year old prisoner prayed, He released her from prison. God listened to their prayers.

God not only saves those people who seek Him but He also heals their souls. He also had me pray a few thousand times for one soul and worked through my prayers. Our God works through our prayers. That is why I cannot help but pray. If I pray, I can even save the lives of those who are dying.

Chapter 4

Sowing Seeds of Love and Blessing in China

I have prayed for Vice Minister Song and Vice Minister Li more than 10,000 times. If we pray for one person with love for a few thousand times, that prayer has power.

Breaking Records in China

The initial list of Chinese friends I put together to intercede for was around 20 people. When I became the Ambassador, the list had expanded to over 40. By the time I was appointed as the Minister of Unification and left Beijing, the list had increased to around 80 people.

In 1995, one of the most important people on my prayer list was Vice Minister Song (pseudonym; he is currently a senior official in China). When I served as the Minister for Political Affairs in the Korean Embassy in Beijing, he was a Deputy Director-General in the Chinese Ministry of Foreign Affairs.

When I returned to Korea to serve as the Director-General of Asia-Pacific Affairs Bureau, he was also promoted to the Director-General level. When I became the Senior Secretary to the President for Foreign Policy and National Security, a Vice Ministerial level, he was also promoted to a Vice Ministerial post. When I went to China, he became a Vice Minister at the Ministry of Foreign Affairs.

When I was appointed as the Ambassador to China on September 10, 2001, the Chinese government accepted my agrément in just one week. Within two days of arriving in Beijing, I presented my credentials to Chinese President Jiang Zemin. It was unprecedented for an Ambassador, anywhere in the world, to present his credentials to the Head of State just two days after arriving at his post (the presentation of credentials normally takes about 15 days to one month). The Chinese Ministry of Foreign Affairs organized the welcoming dinner for me the day after I presented my credentials. This was also an exception as these dinners were usually held at a much later date, sometimes even several months later. The speed with which I was welcomed by the Chinese government set a new record and this was much talked about within the Chinese diplomatic circles.

The person who hosted the welcoming dinner was Vice Minister Song. Vice Minister Song at that time said to me, "I think it's safe to say that you broke all previous records and set a new precedent in the Chinese Ministry of Foreign Affairs!"

The reason I received such warm hospitality from the Ministry of Foreign Affairs was because of the support I had from my friends like Vice Minister Song. The people whom I had been praying for the last few years were all working in influential positions in various areas in China.

Saving a Life Through Prayers of Love

In the beginning of May 2004, I heard that Vice Minister Song fell ill and was hospitalized. I heard that he was going to undergo surgery, but I did not know what the illness was. After I heard this news, I prayed for him daily, and often a few times a day. I kept hearing from others that it would be very difficult for him to fully recover. I prayed even more fervently for Vice Minister Song's healing.

One day when I was praying for him, I received an interpretation of tongues, 'This is not fair! Why are you giving me this illness when I have worked so hard for my country? This is not fair.' Then I received these words in my heart, 'I love him. Do not worry. I will heal him. You need to tell him this.'

I did not know what to do. I could not go and visit him at the hospital and even if I did, I could not tell an atheist in the Communist Party that God said these words. Few days passed by and I received the same words every time I prayed.

I answered God, 'Yes, Lord, I will tell him.'

Although I promised God that I would obey, I still could not get myself to tell Vice Minister Song what I received from God. Then, a few days later as I was praying, I received the same words again. Afterwards, when I was on my way to work, I was suddenly overcome with fear.

'If I do not tell Vice Minister Song soon, God might strike me!'

As soon as I arrived at work, I wrote the following letter in Chinese:

It's been two and a half years since I started working in Beijing. If I did not have your friendship and received your full-fledged support, I would not be leading such a successful term as the Ambassador to China. You are not only important to China but also to me, as you are a dear friend of mine.

I have been praying for you incessantly. When I recently heard that you were ill, I prayed for you several times a day. I cried out to God asking Him to heal you. Recently, I had a feeling that God was speaking to me with these words.

'He blames me for his health. He feels gravely wronged that he became ill when he has worked so hard for his country. But I love him. Do not fear. I will certainly heal him.'

I was relieved to learn that God loves you and that He will protect you. I was comforted knowing that your surgery would go well. Please take care of yourself while you recuperate, and I pray that you will be completely healed soon. I hope to see you working energetically, just like before.

Warmly,
Kim Ha-Joong

I sent the letter. I continued to pray while I waited for Vice

Minister Song's reply. Around ten days later, I received a call.

He said, "Mr. Ambassador, it's me. I was discharged from the hospital yesterday. The surgery went well. I was deeply touched by your letter. Your prayers during this time of hardship have comforted me. Thank you so much."

Praise the Lord! I knelt down to pray thanksgiving to the Lord. Soon afterwards, I hosted a dinner for Vice Minister Song and his wife at our residence, and they came with the staff members of the Foreign Ministry.

Vice Minister Song said, "When I read your letter, I knew I was going to live! I was surprised to see the very words that were written, were the same as the ones I used to complain to the heavens with. I, therefore, believed what you wrote, that I was going to be healed. I keep the letter on my desk in my study."

As the Vice Minister of the Ministry of Foreign Affairs in China, he was a crucial person for Korea. God knew everything and had me intercede for him since 1995. I prayed for him twice a day for the last nine years, which meant that I had prayed for him about 6,000 times. I came to understand that God listens when someone prays for another for a long time with tears and love in their heart.

> And the prayer offered in faith will make the sick person well; the Lord will raise him up. If he has sinned, he will be forgiven. Therefore confess your sins to each other and pray for each other so that

you may be healed. The prayer of a righteous man is powerful and effective. (James 5:15-16)

God truly loves Korea, and because He puts importance on Korea-China relations, God worked in miraculous ways. Vice Minister Song continued to be in influential positions thereafter, and now, he is serving at the Ministerial level in the Chinese government. I still pray for him now, even though it has been more than 19 years since I began to pray for him.

Blessing Others

Li (pseudonym; he is currently a senior official in China) was the Vice Minister at the Chinese Ministry of Foreign Affairs. I met him for the first time on August 24, 1992, which was the historic day when Korea and China established diplomatic relations. Li at the time was the Deputy Director-General of Asian Affairs Bureau in the Chinese Ministry of Foreign Affairs, and was my counterpart when I was serving as the Minister for Political Affairs at the Korean Embassy in Beijing. Li was also one of the first twenty on my list of people to pray for, and remains my close friend for whom I continue to pray even now.

We worked very closely until 1994, when Deputy Director-

General Li was posted as the Minister at the Chinese Embassy in Japan. I returned to Korea as the Director-General of Asia Pacific Affairs Bureau in Seoul and had many opportunities to visit Japan. I met with Li every time I visited Japan. I had already been praying for him every day, and whenever we met, I would tell him the following:

"Minister Li! Come and serve as the Ambassador of China to Korea."

"I cannot because I do not speak Korean." Li would say.

"I have no doubt that you will serve as the Ambassador in Korea." I insisted.

Every time I met him in Japan, I said the same thing.

"In 1998, there will be a new government in Korea. Come to Korea in the fall, and serve as the Ambassador to Korea. I'm praying that this will happen."

In the fall of 1998, Li really did come to Korea as the Chinese Ambassador. At the time, I was the Chief of Protocol to the President, and was later promoted to Senior Secretary to the President for Foreign Policy and National Security. Both of these positions are crucial contacts for any Ambassador serving in Korea. Every time Ambassador Li had a difficult issue, he called me or came to see me. Back then, I did not have time to meet with foreign ambassadors in Korea due to my demanding schedule. I would cordially refuse any meeting requests unless it was very important. However, with Ambassador Li it was different because he was a special friend. He was also on my prayer list, so I tried my best to help him.

In December 2000, my wife and I had dinner with Ambassador Li and his wife. I asked Ambassador Li how long he had been in Korea.

"Two and a half years." He answered.

"Then, it will be three years this coming fall. I think three years have been plenty to serve as the Ambassador to Korea. Next fall, what do you think about becoming the new Ambassador to Japan?" I said smiling at him.

Li shook his head and said, "Oh, no, I can't go as the Ambassador to Japan. The incumbent has only been there for a year and a half. Even if I do go, I would need to wait for another one and a half years. And based on a lot of different reasons, it is just not possible for me to become the Ambassador to Japan right now."

I disagreed. "No, that's not true. I really believe that you will be the next Ambassador to Japan this coming fall."

Ambassador Li was correct when he said that the duration of service for ambassadors is three years, and so he would have to wait another year and half. However, in June 2001, the Chinese Ambassador to Japan was suddenly appointed as the Under Secretary-General at the United Nations and the ambassadorship in Japan became vacant. It was completely unexpected and both Ambassador Li and I were quite surprised. Soon, the Chinese government appointed Ambassador Li as the new Chinese Ambassador to Japan.

Before Ambassador Li moved to Japan, he hosted a dinner for me in Korea. After dinner, I talked to Ambassador Li privately.

"Ambassador Li, go back to Beijing in the fall of 2004 and serve as the Vice Minister at the Ministry of Foreign Affairs."

He looked at me with a surprised look and said, "I can't go back to the Ministry as the Vice Minister! The last time I was at headquarters, I was serving as a Deputy Director-General. How could I go back and become a Vice Minister? That's not possible."

I assured him, "Don't worry. It will happen."

He went to Japan and soon afterwards, I was appointed as the Ambassador to China. In the fall of 2004, I heard a rumor that one of the Vice Ministers in the Chinese Ministry of Foreign Affairs was soon to be appointed as the Ambassador to Japan.

Immediately, I thought, 'Ambassador Li must be coming to fill in the vacant post!'

I called Ambassador Li and asked him.

"Ambassador Li, are you coming back to Beijing? Are you coming back as the Vice Minister?"

Ambassador Li answered, "Ambassador Kim, I'm afraid I'm not returning to the Ministry of Foreign Affairs."

I was puzzled and asked, "Why?"

"I'm going somewhere else."

"Oh really? Do you remember what I said to you in Seoul?"

"Yes, I do." He said.

"Do you believe it?"

Ambassador Li answered, "No, I don't because I cannot go back to the Ministry of Foreign Affairs."

I then asked him, "When are you coming back?"

"In three weeks time."

Finally, I said to him, "Okay, three more weeks. We have time. Let's see what happens." and we hung up.

Two weeks after this phone conversation, there was a sudden change. Ambassador Li was appointed as the Vice Minister for Foreign Affairs. I was stunned and so was Ambassador Li. Even though I had said those things, I marveled that what I said had come to pass all three times.

I worked with Vice Minister Li for three and a half years until I left China to serve as the Minister of Unification. Vice Minister Li always gave me his full support. All of this was possible because of our friendship that began in 1992, which blossomed while he served as the Ambassador to Korea.

In March 2005, then Deputy Secretary General of the Korean National Security Council Lee Jong-Seok informally visited China. When he arrived, Lee had a meeting and a luncheon with Vice Minister Li.

During the luncheon, Deputy Secretary General Lee asked Vice Minister Li, "I heard that you and Ambassador Kim Ha-

Joong are very close. How would you describe your relationship?"

Vice Minister Li answered, "There are several people who can call me after midnight. It is the Director-General of Asia Affairs Bureau and the Director of Korean Peninsula Affairs at the Ministry of Foreign Affairs. The third person is Ambassador Kim. I have a personal mobile phone and only a few people, including my wife, know this number. Ambassador Kim is one of them. Is that a sufficient description of our friendship?"

Please Extend His Retirement Age

Vice Minister Li was born in December 1946; he was born two weeks earlier than me. According to the lunar calendar, we were both born in the Year of the Dog. Our closeness in age helped us bond.

In China, government employees retire at the age of sixty. According to regulation, Vice Minister Li had to retire in December 2006. Since he was assigned a very important task, I was wondering whether he could indeed retire.

Since the beginning of 2006, I had been praying to God to extend Vice Minister Li's retirement age. December came and there was still no word that Vice Minister Li would retire as the regulations stipulated. I continued to pray. One day, Vice Minister Li called and suggested that we meet on December 28. On the day we were going to meet I prayed to God.

'Lord, you know that I have been praying the entire year that you would extend his retirement age. Please, extend his retirement age.'

God answered. 'He will be there for a while.'

I wrote down those words on a piece of paper and went to meet Vice Minister Li. The meeting was about the Six Party Talks. After the meeting, I asked him about his retirement.

"What happened to your retirement? 2006 is almost over."

He smiled and said, "It has been extended."

I asked, "For how long?"

"For a while."

When I heard him say 'a while' I showed him the words I had written down that morning. I had translated 'a while' into Chinese. I told him that I had prayed for him that morning and God told me that he would be there for 'a while.' He was surprised and his colleagues, who were there, were also taken aback.

On the way back to the Embassy, I read the prayer to First Secretary Kim Geon and Second-Secretary Yeo So-Young.

When I met with Vice Minister Li afterwards, I asked him.

"How long is 'a while'?"

"I'd say about six months."

I told him, "God's 'while' is not that kind of a while. It's at least one, two or even three years."

"Impossible! Our government's 'while' is about six months."

That was in the end of December 2006 and Vice Minister Li resigned from Vice Ministership in January 2010, but he is still working for the government and playing a very important role.

I have prayed countless number of times for Vice Minister Li. I prayed for him for three years after I told him to come to Korea as the Ambassador, and he was appointed as the Ambassador to Korea. I told him that he would go to Japan as the Ambassador and continued to pray, and he really did go as the Ambassador to Japan.

After three years, I told him that he should come and serve as the Vice Minister, and when I prayed, he was appointed as the Vice Minister. I also prayed that God would extend his retirement age, and God extended that as well. God answers prayers when one prays for his friend.

I have prayed for Vice Minister Song and Vice Minister Li more than 10,000 times. If we pray for one person with love for a few thousand times, that prayer has power. Some people might think that I was able to serve a long time as the Ambassador to China because I was good at networking.

Rather, it was the dream I had for China that was birthed in 1965 while I was studying Chinese literature, and the endless hours of prayer that I prayed for my friends in China since 1995, that granted me success. These are the real reasons why I was able to be in China as the longest serving Korean Ambassador, which is the longest time a Korean career diplomat served in one country.

Talking About Love

In the beginning of 2005, the Beijing Television Broadcast Company (BTV) requested that I appear for a television program called "TV with You." This program had been on the air for fifteen years and it was one of the most beloved programs in Beijing. It was selected as the viewers' favorite program for nine consecutive years.

The broadcast company had planned a special series entitled 'Conversations with Ambassadors in China.' They were going to record interviews with 30 of the 170 Ambassadors serving in China and they were planning to broadcast one interview a week. I asked God whether I should appear in the program. God told me to go ahead, and He said, 'You will reveal my glory through this program.'

I wondered how I was going to glorify God by appearing in a Chinese television program but I decided to obey God's words.

The TV station informed me that our first recording would be at my residence, and then the second one would be at the studio. A lady, who was the emcee of the program, arrived at my residence with the production crew. As the emcee of a popular program, she was one of the most famous media personalities in China.

I prayed for the emcee the night before the first recording. God suddenly, in my heart, told me, 'She is a lonely person, so talk to her about love.'

After the recording at the residence, we served lunch to the emcee, the producer and the camera crew. The Public Relations Officer at the Korean Embassy also joined us for lunch.

We were having an informal conversation during the luncheon when the emcee asked me, "Mr. Ambassador, what do you think is the most important thing in the world? Is it money? Is it power? Or is it honor?"

I answered, "I think love is the most important."

"What? Love?"

She looked at the producer who was sitting next to her and said, "Love?" and laughed. She was clearly surprised to hear such an answer from an Ambassador.

I looked at her and said, "Is there anything you do not have? You obviously have fame; you are a beautiful woman and I assume you have money. But, you don't have love, do you?"

She was alarmed and asked me, "What do you mean? Who said that?"

"God did. I prayed for you yesterday and God told me that you feel alone. God also told me to talk to you about love."

She froze when I said those words and she stopped eating. I did not know at the time that she was a divorcée. The atmosphere became awkward so we hurried to finish the luncheon and parted our ways.

I went to the studio on the day of the recording. I was standing next to the emcee before going up on stage and she said to me, "Mr. Ambassador, I could not sleep at all that night. But what you told me has been a big help. I will always cherish your words deep in my heart."

> He reveals deep and hidden things; he knows what lies in darkness, and light dwells with him. (Daniel 2:22)

The Multitalented Ambassador

When we were recording at the residence, the emcee had a request.

She said, "When our viewers picture an Ambassador, they always think of a black car with a flag, and parties with wine. They think Ambassadors are different from the average citizen. We need to do something unique so that the audience feels closer to you." Then, she asked me, "Do you sing well, Mr. Ambassador?"

"Well, I don't sing that well but I do know how to sing."

"Do you play any instrument?"

I told her, "I play the guitar."

The emcee was pleased and asked me, "Wonderful! Do you think you can you play the guitar and sing in front of the audience at the studio?"

I thought for a moment and answered, "Sure, why not?"

When I was a student of Chinese literature at Seoul National University, my friends and I put together a vocal group called 'The EXTAS'. It was one of the very first college bands in Korea, and I was the lead guitarist. We performed in numerous concerts back then so I did have a lot of experience when it came to going on stage and performing. There was a song I used to sing a lot as well, but in more private settings. It was 'Have I Told You Lately That I Love You' by Patti Page, which was a song very popular in Korea during the 1960s. I had translated the song into Korean. This song became very popular among the young people. Later in the 1980s, I found out that the Korean version of the song was included in a songbook and it said 'by an anonymous adapter.' I had been thinking of registering my name as the adapter of the song but have not been able to until now.

I planned to sing this song in the studio so I translated the lyrics into Chinese. This was because I thought that the audience might like it better if I sang it in Chinese rather than English or Korean.

After the emcee and I talked to each other backstage, the recording began. There were about 100 Chinese people in the audience and Mr. Wi Gye-Chool, the Minister for Public Relations in the Korean Embassy (later Ambassador to Ghana) was also in the audience. During the recording, the time had come for me to sing. I gave a brief introduction of the song before I played the song.

"This song is originally an American song and I adapted the song into Korean in the 1960s."

The emcee asked me to sing it in English. After I finished singing, the emcee asked me to sing it in Korean. After I finished singing in Korean, she asked me, "Mr. Ambassador, can you sing it in Chinese?"

I said, "Yes." When I sang the song in Chinese, the audience cheered and gave me a big round of applause.

The recording proceeded smoothly. We filmed speaking in Chinese for over an hour; I never had a "no good" scene. The emcee said that while she had moderated the program for over 10 years, this was the first time that the filming was completed without a single "no good" scene. I thanked God, as I knew that this was only possible because He gave me courage and wisdom throughout the interview.

The filming of the 30 Ambassadors continued for the next few months. On November 30, the broadcast company held a press launch before the show 'Conversations with Ambassadors in China' was aired. All the Ambassadors who took part in this program participated in the press launch along with various Chinese artists and media personnel. At this press launch, I received 'The Best Multitalented Ambassador Award' from the broadcast company for my fluency in Chinese and the diversity of topics that were broached during my interview.

Glorifying God

The Beijing Television Broadcast Company (BTV) announced the following before the program was aired.

> On December 1, the 'Conversations with Ambassadors in China' will air. The first segment is titled 'The Korean Ambassador's Love for China'. Ambassador Kim, who is fluent in Chinese, has a great sense of humor. He shared his life stories with the audience and revealed that he 'submits to his wife'.
>
> Because of the time limit, we could not include all the scenes where Ambassador Kim expressed his love for the Chinese people. The scenes from this segment show that both the audience and Ambassador Kim do not cease to laugh. The producers had a difficult time leaving out certain scenes when editing the program. In the last part of the program, the multitalented Ambassador Kim played the guitar and sang a song in English,

Korean and Chinese. Through this song, we were able to see the affectionate and authentic side of Ambassador Kim.

On December 1, my portion of the program was aired. BTV is the largest broadcast company in Beijing and it is estimated that millions of people watch BTV; however, even BTV was surprised how overwhelmingly positive the viewers of my segment responded. Therefore in 2006, during Chinese New Year, which is China's biggest holiday, BTV re-aired the program during it's golden hour with the title, 'The Korean Ambassador Reignites Korean Fever'.

According to BTV, after the program was aired, they provided the recorded tapes to thousands of buildings, agencies and landlords who showed the program on the televisions in their buildings' lobbies, corridors and elevators.

Later, when I met an influential Chinese media personnel, he said, "Many who work in the media were greatly surprised by the overwhelming response from the Chinese viewers to your part of the program. A few days ago, I was talking about this to my friend. I asked whether he had any ideas as to why your program was so popular. My friend said, 'People are saying the Korean Ambassador is successful because the God who the Korean Ambassador believes in protects him and blesses him.'

I was surprised. "It is hard to believe that the Chinese people would say such a thing. . ."

First, the Chinese people did not know me, and second, it was hard to imagine that the people would talk about God in a society like China.

However, when I met with Mr. Ahn Soo-Hoon (pseudonym) when visiting the Jiangsu province in March 2006, I was deeply moved by what Mr. Ahn said to me.

"I have recently met many Chinese Christians. I was startled to hear from them that many Chinese Christians pray for you. They were touched that the Korean Ambassador who is a Christian prays for their own country and people. They were also encouraged that you share the gospel with people from different walks of life in China and bravely testify that God is alive. You have been the talk of the town and many of the Chinese Christians are praying for you."

When I learned this I realized that the Chinese media personnel's words were true. I only then remembered what God told me, "You will reveal my glory through this program." I knelt down and gave a prayer of thanksgiving to God.

> Arise, shine, for your light has come, and the glory of the Lord rises upon you. (Isaiah 60:1)

Love for the Chinese People

In May 28, 2005, I headed a trade and investment mission and cultural troupe of over 170 people to Chongqing. We went to participate in the "Korea-Chongqing City's Korea-China Friendship Week" festival. The Korea-China Friendship Week is an event co-organized by the Korean Embassy and provincial government.

This event is held twice a year in capitals of different provinces, and the objective of the event is to promote cultural exchange and economic cooperation between Korea and the local governments.

That evening, I held a meeting with the Koreans who work and reside in Chongqing. Approximately 15 people including the Representative of the Korean Association in Chongqing attended. During the meeting, one person stood up and spoke to me in an angry voice.

"Mr. Ambassador! I took over a boiler factory after I came here. I collaborated with the Chinese companies to take over the company in the form of a joint venture. The Chinese companies invested 22 percent and I invested 78 percent. After investing so much money, the factory is running quite well, and now my Chinese partners are trying to oust me. This does not make any sense! Please do something!"

After he was done talking, I said to him, "As the Ambassador and a China specialist, having listened to what you just said, I don't think you can do business here in China. If you continue to be suspicious of your Chinese partners, it will not be possible for you to succeed here in China. This applies to everyone who is present here. If you want to do business in China, you need to love China and the Chinese people."

After the meeting, we moved to the dinner reception hall. The man, who was angry during the meeting, came to my table during dinner.

"Mr. Ambassador, I wish to apologize for losing my temper in front of so many people. My name is Lim Sung-Ryong."

"Mr. Lim, even if you are angry, you need to love the Chinese people. You should not blurt out your thoughts like that. Have you ever prayed?"

"No, I have not."

"All right, then please pray tonight. Please kneel down and say 'Lord, I love China. I love the Chinese people. I love those who do business with me.' 50 percent of your problems will be resolved just by praying."

The next morning, when I saw Mr. Lim, I asked, "Have you prayed?"

"Yes, I did."

"All right. Half of your problems have been resolved."

In the morning, our delegation met with the Mayor of Chongqing (Ministerial level) and negotiated many different issues. I also briefed the Mayor about the boiler factory issue and asked him to look into it. In the evening, we were invited to a dinner hosted by the Mayor. The Mayor called in a city official and told him to give me an update on the boiler factory situation.

The official briefed me. "I have looked into the situation and took some corrective measures. Half of the problems have been resolved."

When I heard that 'half of the problems have been resolved' I immediately asked for Mr. Lim. I asked the same official to update him on the situation. The official repeated the same thing. It was clear that Mr. Lim was deeply moved. After dinner I said to Mr. Lim, "I told you yesterday. If you love the Chinese people, 50 percent of your problems would be resolved."

Mr. Lim nodded in agreement.

I asked Mr. Lim, "Where is your boiler factory? I want to go to your factory tomorrow."

He answered, "Mr. Ambassador, I don't think you can come. The factory is far away."

When I asked the city officials, they said that the factory was located in a place where there was no paved roads and difficult for cars to drive through. I was determined to go all the more when I heard that it was difficult to get there.

"I still want to go."

I also instructed my staff to request the city government to invite as many press as possible to accompany our visit to the factory.

A Company Raised with Love

The next day, we headed to the factory. When we got out of the car, our foots sank into the mud. Many of Chongqing City's press were present to cover the story of the Korean Ambassador walking through the muddy road to visit the Chinese factory. We went into the office after looking around the factory. Mr. Lim's joint venture investors were waiting for me. The newspaper and television reporters followed me into the office. I sat down to hear the company's updates.

After the briefing, in front of the television cameras, I said, "These days, many Korean businessmen come to China and do business with the Chinese people. I hear there are cases where the partners work well together in the beginning, but the Chinese partners break promises and kick out the Koreans to overtake the business once it starts doing well. I believe that this never happens in Chongqing. When I spoke to the Mayor of Chongqing and the Party Secretary, they promised to protect the Korean businesses."

I looked at Mr. Lim and continued, "Mr. Lim, your partners who are here are not such people. Please do not be suspicious of them and please love them. Then, they will help you. There are so many reporters from Chongqing here and they are watching us. What you are worried about will not happen. If something strange happens, I will come back to Chongqing again and talk to my close friends, the Mayor and the Party Secretary and ask for their cooperation."

I then asked the Chinese partners to say something. They said that they would continue to work closely with their Korean partner. I took a group picture and came outside. Before I left, I talked to Mr. Lim.

"80 percent of your problems have been resolved. The remaining 20 percent will depend on your prayers. When you pray, the 20 percent will be filled. But if you do not pray, it will not be filled. Will you pray?"

Mr. Lim nodded and told me, "Yes, Mr. Ambassador, I will pray."

I received a call from Mr. Lim a while later. The Chinese partners offered him compensation and asked Mr. Lim to sell the factory to them. When I heard the compensation conditions, I advised Mr. Lim that he should accept and not be too greedy about it. Afterwards, Mr. Lim called me and said that he received full compensation and was able to move on.

"Mr. Ambassador, thank you very much. I don't know how to repay you for your help. Please tell me what to do. I will do anything you tell me to do."

I said, "Please go to church, and believe in God. I do not want anything more than that."

Mr. Lim agreed and hung up the phone.

The pastor at the Chongqing Korean Church later told me that

Mr. Lim started coming to church with his family. Mr. Lim sent me an email through the pastor.

> "Thanks to you, I was able to resolve the business issue. When I asked you how I could repay you, you told me that you did not need anything except that I would attend church. It was the most difficult thing for me to do. Even as I risked losing everything, I did not for one moment think that I should rely on God. Because of your help, I was able to resolve the issue but more importantly, I was able to accept Jesus Christ as my Savior. Every time, I get lazy in my faith, I think about the gratitude I felt at that time. Our family will live a life of victory in Jesus Christ."

God is a faithful God. He sent me to Chongqing to help Mr. Lim who was facing a crisis and eventually led him to believe in Him. I do not know how Mr. Lim changed, as a few years have already passed since I received his email; however, I sincerely believe that he continues to be deeply moved by God's grace, and therefore, is in close relationship with God. Mr. Lim probably still continues to love China and the Chinese people, and in return is loved by them.

Chapter 5

God Uses Those Who Pray and Listen to Him

She began to change from that day forward and became a prayer warrior. The fact that God knew whether she prayed and how much she prayed seemed to transform her and added fire to her prayer life.

Let Her Go

When I was appointed as the Ambassador to China, there was a Korean secretary named Miss Song in the Ambassador's office. Having held the same position under the previous Ambassador, she continued as my administrative assistant. While I was praying one morning, in the beginning of July 2004, God told me to "let her go."

After I arrived at the office that day, I called my assistant First Secretary Kim Han-Kyu and asked how long Miss Song had been working at the office. Mr. Kim told me that she had been working there for four years. When I asked how often local staff were moved around the different administrative offices, he told me that they normally moved every two years. I then told him to transfer her since she had been there twice as long as the average person. I also advised him to move her along with other employees who had been there for more than two years, since it might draw unnecessary attention if she were the only personnel moved. I asked him to speak to her about this by the end of the day.

That day, like any other day, I returned to the office after having lunch. Miss Song entered my office with coffee, but after she placed the coffee on the table, she did not leave.

"Miss Song, do you have something to tell me?" I asked.

"Yes, Mr. Ambassador. I'd like to talk to you about something."

"What is it?" I asked.

"Mr. Ambassador, I wish to leave this office." She replied.

"Did Mr. Kim say anything to you?" I asked.

"No, did you say something to Mr. Kim?" She asked in return.

"Then, why do you want to leave?" I asked again.

She explained, "When you were appointed as the Ambassador to China in the fall of 2001, I thought you might stay just a little over a year, so I told my parents in Korea that I would leave China when you left. However, it has been over three years since your appointment, and it doesn't look like you will be leaving anytime soon. My parents are now becoming very impatient waiting for my return to Korea so I can get married. I've been agonizing over this decision for several days, and wanted to speak with you about it."

I called Mr. Kim into the office and asked him to repeat what I had told him in the morning. Both Mr. Kim and Miss Song were very surprised. Miss Song was a Christian. God knew what was on Miss Song's heart and He had told me to "let her go" in advance just in case I would not be responsive to Miss Song's words alone.

Miss Song returned to Korea in mid-July.

Jesus Already Knows

Miss Song had a sister who was a missionary in the Middle East. I had never met her sister, but occasionally sent funds to support her sister's work. In mid-May 2005, about ten months after Miss Song had left for Korea, I was praying and felt that God wanted me to send some money to Miss Song's sister.

I learned her bank account number from Miss Song in Korea and sent a monetary gift. Shortly after, I received a phone call from Miss Song. She told me that her sister was a self-supporting missionary, and had run out of money. She had been praying to God when she received my contribution. Miss Song was in tears as she relayed her sister's gratitude.

A few days later, I received an email from Miss Song's sister. She wrote:

> "I am deeply humbled by the fact that even as you are carrying out incredibly important work for our country, you are so dependent on the One above and so sensitive to the Holy Spirit's leading. I promise to pray for you, and like you, will strive to listen to His voice. I cannot help but be incredibly thankful that

God has given such a Spirit-filled intercessor to someone as small and weak as me. I firmly believe that those who pray in the Spirit are doing the work of God.

Please do not worry about material concerns for us. We chose to be self-supporting missionaries, deciding to depend as little as possible on others - though, of course, God's leading is more important than any decisions we make. Because God has allowed it, we receive your offering gladly. Truthfully, we were facing some financial difficulty lately, so what you sent was an enormous help to us. God really knows us and our circumstances!

I pray that you will always be dependent on the leading of the Holy Spirit and be full of joy and blessing."

About a year after I received that message, I was praying one morning when God gave me a word about Miss Song's sister, even though I was not praying for her at the time. In general, the words I received from Him for her were the following:

"You've been there too long; you should move."

I called Miss Song in Seoul and relayed the words to her, telling Miss Song that her sister would know what the words I received during prayer meant.

Not even an hour had passed when Miss Song called me after speaking to her sister. Sobbing, she said, "Ambassador, my sister had been wrestling in prayer about the decision to move for some time. Recently, her work became dangerous and difficult, and she felt spiritually oppressed. But when she heard your words, she received fresh encouragement and wanted me to relay to you her gratefulness." Miss Song continued and said that everything was a moving witness to her about God's love and that she was literally shaking from excitement.

I emailed her sister the impressions I had from God during prayer, and received the following reply from her husband.

> "Each word you wrote touched us to the core. Recently, there have been many difficult days, so we were praying for help. We truly believe that the Holy Spirit sent us the answers to our prayers through you."

Later, Miss Song asked me in wonder, "Mr. Ambassador! How could this kind of thing happen?"

"It is because we worship a Living God." I replied.

With these two incidents, Miss Song came to believe more than ever that God was a real presence in our lives.

Miss Kim, the Prayer Warrior

When Miss Song left for Korea, the General Affairs Office gave me the names of two potential candidates to fill her position. One was named Miss Cho and the other was named Miss Kim. When I asked God about which one to choose, I felt God preferred Miss Cho to Miss Kim.

I contacted the administrative offices and asked whether Miss Cho would be open to working in the Ambassador's office. But I was told that she had recently gotten engaged and would be leaving the Embassy soon.

I went to God in prayer again, and asked whether I should choose Miss Kim instead for the position. 'No,' He said. I asked whether I should choose someone else. 'No,' He said again.

'Then what should I do? Why can't I choose Miss Kim?' I asked.

'She believes in Me but she doesn't pray,' He replied.

The next day, I called Miss Kim into the office.

"Miss Kim, do you believe in Jesus?" I asked.

"Yes," she said.

"Do you pray?" I asked.

"Yes," she replied.

"Really? I believe you do not pray."

"How do you know?" She asked, surprised to hear me contradict her own words.

When I shared what I had heard during prayer, she admitted, in tears, "I'm so sorry. Actually, I have not been praying."

When I checked her file, I learned that her father was a pastor. I asked her.

"Miss Kim, how can you not pray when you are the daughter of a minister? I think God wants your prayers. Miss Kim, will you pray and work in the Ambassador's office or will you continue to not pray and not work here?" I asked.

"I will pray," she said.

"Can you promise?" I asked.

"I promise," she said.

"Great!" I replied. "Then I will request the appointment."

A few months after Miss Kim began to work in the Ambassador's office, I was curious as to whether Miss Kim was praying, so I asked God.

'Lord, does Miss Kim pray?'

'No.'

The next day, I called her into the office and asked, "Miss Kim, are you praying?" When she did not answer, I asked why she was not praying when she had promised that she would.

She began to cry and said, "I will."

She Prays a Little

A few months later, I asked God about Miss Kim again.

'God, is Miss Kim praying these days?'

'A little bit.'

When Miss Kim came into the office to serve coffee the next day, I asked her whether she was praying these days. When she said that she did, I asked her whether it was just a little. Taken aback, she stared at me.

I said, "God says that you are praying, but just a little."

She began sobbing at those words. The tears seemed to be ones of fear, repentance and thanksgiving to the One who knew her so well.

She began to change from that day forward and became a prayer warrior. The fact that God knew whether she prayed and how much she prayed seemed to transform her and added fire to her prayer life.

> From heaven the Lord looks down and sees all mankind; from his dwelling place he watches all who live on earth - he who forms the hearts of all, who considers everything they do. (Psalm 33:13-15)

As Miss Kim began to pray more earnestly, her faith grew in a way and at a speed that even surprised me. Her actions and tone were not those of her former self. I asked her one day whether she prayed much. Her bold and confident answer in the affirmative seemed to reflect her new spiritual strength and steadfastness.

Go to a New Place!

In May of 2006, while I was praying, God told me, in my heart, to send Miss Kim to a different place. After lunch, I asked her how long she had been working at our office.

"It has been 22 months," she replied.

"Then, it's time to go to a different place." I told her.

As soon as I spoke those words, she put her head on my desk and began to cry. She told me that she had recently attended a revival service where a pastor had prayed for her and had told her, "It's now time to leave this place." She had already been wondering to where and how she would leave, by the time I spoke those words to her.

I also wondered where I should send this prayer warrior. At the time, there was a diplomat in the Consular Office who had been doing a wonderful job of taking care of North Korean asylum seekers. The job required the person in the position to genuinely love the North Koreans. However, that diplomat was slated to return to Korea in the fall. In looking for a replacement, no one had come to mind who was devoted to clothing, feeding, and listening sympathetically and patiently to the complaints and needs of the asylum seekers.

I told God that I would send Miss Kim to this position, and God affirmed my decision. He also gave me words for her.

God Uses Those Who Are Prepared

At the end of May, Miss Kim was to go to the Consular Office. I thanked her for all her efforts at the Ambassador's office and gave her the words that God gave me for her:

My Beloved Daughter, You are my daughter whom I love.
I know that your heart is full of love
and thanksgiving toward Me.
I am proud of you.
I see that you stand in front of Me,
deeply rooted in your faith.
You are going to do many good things for Me,
leading many people to Me.
Many wondrous things will happen through you.
Your petitions will be answered
and what you say will come to pass.
You are a strong woman.

What you say with conviction will not be easily ignored,
so continue to tell others about Me.
Then, your surroundings will be changed.
Now go to a new place and transform it.
When you intercede for others with your tears,
you will see great and amazing things come to pass.
Others' hearts will be transformed as you pray for them.
Then, you will know that it was already all in My plans.
Continue to pray.
And rely only on Me.
Then, I will bless you mightily,
and I will do great things through you.
You are a daughter whom I love.
I love you deeply.

Miss Kim sobbed as she read those words. Soon after, she moved to the Consular Office.

A short while after Miss Kim began her work, the diplomat in charge of the North Korean asylum seekers came to me and said, "Mr. Ambassador, I have been praying to God for months for Him to send someone deeply rooted in prayer. So I was grateful to find that you had sent a prayer warrior like Miss Kim to us!"

Then, I realized why God had sent Miss Kim to me, it was to be trained in prayer for 22 months, before sending her to the Consular

Office. She became an expert on the job, taking care of the North Koreans, helping them and consoling them warmly and wholeheartedly. She had taken on a job that usually goes to a career diplomat and had carried it out successfully.

After Miss Kim had moved to the Consular Office, her father who was a pastor came to visit me and said with emotion,

"Mr. Ambassador, I came to thank you and express my appreciation for what you have done for my daughter. I have been speaking to her for a long time about the need to pray, but you did what even I, as a pastor, couldn't do. You transformed her into a prayer warrior."

"Thank you, but I didn't do it. God did."

It was true. How could I have known whether she prayed or not, or how much or how little she prayed? My guess is that the prayers of her parents and her church community had reached the Heavens. God sent her to me in response to their prayers and He prepared her for the work he had in mind for her.

I got an opportunity to see Miss Kim again just recently. She had left the Consular Office of the Embassy and was getting a graduate degree. I asked her if she was praying much and was happy to hear that she was praying quite a bit. I told her that she was no longer just a prayer warrior but a prayer leader.

In reply, she told me that she thought of me as her spiritual father, who not only challenged her spiritually but also gave her the opportunity and the motivation to change, and that she would always keep me in her prayers. With a firm conviction that only comes through prayer, she is currently devoting herself to her studies. I have every confidence that she will bring even more glory to God with the work that she will do in the future.

The Best Chinese Interpreter

I was able to successfully accomplish my mission as the Ambassador to China because of the tireless dedication and support given to me by my staff. Over 200 career diplomats, countless administrative assistants, secretaries and various helpers were my sources of strength and pride. Everyone worked hard, but one particular diplomat impressed me the most.

Her name is Ms. Yeo, a career diplomat. She came with an unusual academic background, having attended Chinese school in Korea for 12 years, from primary school onwards. She also received her Bachelor's and Master's degrees in Comparative Politics from the Taiwan National University in Taipei. Obviously, she had been preparing to be an expert on China from an early age.

Ever since she was selected to be the official Chinese interpreter for the Korean President in 1999, she was known to be the best interpreter of Chinese in Korea. As reported repeatedly in many newspapers, many Chinese diplomats, including Premier Wen Jiabao, considered her the best speaker of Chinese amongst non-native speakers.

Ms. Yeo was a person of deep faith. She did whatever work was assigned to her without complaint, no matter how difficult the assignment was. During the time I was Ambassador, she was the one who stayed up the greatest number of nights working. During the four years that I worked with her, I got to know her as someone who was wholly devoted to God and His words.

Praying for the Unification of Korea for 19 Years

When I became the Minister of Unification, I came to learn that the position, unlike that of other Ministers, had a special mandate to appoint two policy assistants to serve under me. I considered filling one of these posts with a diplomat from the Ministry of Foreign Affairs and Trade. The delicate issue of unification often needed to be seen from an international perspective, and therefore, coordination with the Ministry of Foreign Affairs and Trade was paramount. However, governmental policy dictated that the policy assistants could not be appointed from among the career diplomats, and could be offered only as a special appointment or by contract.

I was at a loss because most of the diplomats I was considering were regular ministry employees and could not be temporarily moved to another office. The only choice I had was to appoint someone like Ms. Yeo, who was a specialist. I asked Counsellor Seo Doo-Hyun at the Korean Embassy in China, who had accompanied me to Seoul from Beijing, about his opinion on the matter of bringing Ms. Yeo as one of the policy assistants.

Strangely, he did not immediately give an answer but sat in silence. When I asked him why he was not saying anything, he told me the following in response.

"When you asked the question, I felt as though my heart had stopped and all the hairs on my body stood up. Actually, Ms. Yeo had stopped by my office several times last year, asking for an opportunity to work in the Ministry of Unification, even for a little bit. I told her that it was premature for her to ask, given that her rank was not senior enough to request a transfer, according to government regulation. When I asked her why she was interested in even a temporary position at the Ministry, she said that she had been praying for 19 years for the unification of Korea, since she was in the 8th grade. She said that she wrote her master's thesis on the unification of Korea. So when I heard you were considering her as a possible candidate for the position, I just knew that she had been prepared for the post."

I called Ms. Yeo to my office and asked her to share her story. She repeated the same story that Mr. Seo told me. I asked the Minister of Foreign Affairs and Trade for a special permission to bring Ms. Yeo to the Ministry of Unification for a short period, and asked that she be able to return when I left the Ministry. The Ministry of Foreign Affairs and Trade agreed.

During my year at the Ministry of Unification, Ms. Yeo helped me tremendously. I remain thankful to this day that God had heard her prayers of 19 years and sent her to assist me. I am also thankful that she interceded for me and the Korean Embassy in Beijing for a long time.

In a time when most people are concerned about the things of this world, Ms. Yeo prayed with tears, focusing on the needs of her country and her people. I wait expectantly for God to work through her greatly in the future.

Guardian Eagle

There was a follower of God named Ju Mi-Hee (pseudonym) in the southern region of China. We called her Mrs. Ju. She taught Korean and was zealously devoted to serving God. After meeting her and being moved by her faithfulness, I began to intercede for her every day.

On the night of June 18, 2005, while praying for her, I began to say desperately, 'Father, what should I do? How could something like this happen to me? What should I do?'

I ceased praying immediately and called Mrs. Ju to ask whether anything in particular happened. She replied that nothing had happened but thanked me anyway.

The next night, the same prayer came out of my mouth as I was praying for her. So I stopped praying again and called her.

"Mrs. Ju, something has happened, right?"

"Yes," she replied. "In fact, I had called you twice today but was not able to reach you. Something happened in my family a couple of days ago, and I have been worrying about it. When I received your call last night, I didn't say anything and acted as though nothing was wrong, but I began to feel like I should tell you the truth, so I decided to return your call."

She then proceeded to tell me about her worries. It turned out to be something that could happen to any family. I advised her not to panic and to take care of the matter boldly, but first, to call together a group of intercessors and pray. I also continued to pray for her.

A few days later, as I was praying for Mrs. Ju, I got the feeling that the problem was starting to be resolved. When I called Mrs. Ju, she told me that indeed, the issue was beginning to take care of itself. Two days later, I received the following email from Mrs. Ju:

"I felt so strengthened when I learned that you were praying for ordinary people like us, in spite of how busy you must be. After receiving your call, my son fasted for five days and I fasted for three days, fighting our spiritual battle, and afterwards, felt much peace.

My son fell asleep for a little bit while praying and dreamt that two pigeons flew by our house, one landing on our living room window and another on the window sill of my husband's office. Then he saw a giant eagle landing on our roof, standing guard; and he understood that eagle to be you. My son told me that he had received the answer to our prayers.

As a result of this event, we were led to examine ourselves more closely and become more humble. Most importantly, we really experienced Jesus."

I am Not Praying

One year later in the night of May 20, 2006, I was praying for Mrs. Ju again when suddenly, I fell to my side. Then, my body began to writhe and become stiff. Startled, I called Mrs. Ju immediately.

"Mrs. Ju, what are you doing right now?"

"I'm lying down," she said.

"Why are you lying down? Shouldn't you be praying?"

"I'm not praying," she said.

"Why not?" I asked.

"I don't want to pray," she replied.

"How can a believer of God not want to pray?"

"I don't know," she said.

"I was just praying for you when I fell to my side. Then, my body became stiff and I felt paralyzed."

"What?" She asked in surprise. "What do you mean?" She began to cry and shared, "Recently my second son, who is in the army, hurt his back after a car accident. The doctors at the military hospital are telling him to undergo surgery for a ruptured disc, but my son prayed and said that he felt he shouldn't receive surgery, but wait instead.

The military hospital doctors are telling him to have the surgery, but my son is wanting to get physical therapy from a civilian hospital. We've been in China for 10 years, so we don't have any health insurance or the money to go to Korea to visit our son. The only thing I can do is pray.

I had just received a phone call from my son, who was crying while telling me that he will have to undergo surgery in a few days. I felt frustrated to only be praying in response to such an immense problem.

I was so exhausted, even praying was difficult, so I just decided to lay down. And as I began telling God, 'If my son dies, he will be buried in the national cemetery; if he lives, he will do Your work. I really don't care,' my body started to become stiff. It was exactly at that moment that I got your call."

When I heard those words, I felt a chill go down my spine. I told Mrs. Ju that I would help, and to not worry but be faithful in prayer. While praying intensely for her son, I also assured her that he would not require surgery.

The next day, I went to the office and told the Defense Attaché in the Embassy to contact the military hospital in Korea, where Mrs. Ju's son was staying, and to find out about his current condition. I also asked him whether it was possible to get Mrs. Ju's son physical therapy at a civilian hospital, given that he was young and he himself did not want the surgery. I also added that since his parents are living a hard life in China, it would be good to have him receive any help the military hospital could provide.

A bit later, I received the report from the Attaché. After finding out about Mrs. Ju's son's exact condition, the military hospital agreed to release him to receive physical therapy without surgery at a civilian hospital. I gave thanks to God after hearing the news. His back healed after undergoing physical therapy, and ultimately, did not need to receive surgery.

Mrs. Ju loved God and He held her precious in His sight. So whenever she experienced hardship, He used me to communicate with her, to give her strength and courage. This was an amazing experience of how God cherishes those He loves as the apple of His eye.

> Keep me as the apple of your eye; hide me in the shadow of your wings. (Psalm 17:8)

God Who Helps Those in Need

In mid-March of 2006, I went on a business trip to Nanjing in Jiangsu Province. While preparing for the trip, someone named Ahn Soo-Hoon (pseudonym), who lived in the vicinity of Shanghai, called me at the Ambassador's office. He said that he was working for God, and that he wanted to meet me if I ever came to Nanjing. When I went to God to ask whether I should meet him, God advised me to see him. God also gave me the thought of giving Mr. Ahn a monitary gift. When I told God the amount I was thinking of giving him, God told me to give him more. So I told God that I would give him twice the amount I was originally thinking of giving him.

I prepared the money in $100 bills. I gave the money to my assistant Second Secretary Kang Hyung-Shik, and asked him to give it to me when I was in Nanjing. After arriving in Jiangsu

Province, I set up an appointment to have breakfast together with Mr. Ahn.

Before leaving for breakfast, I asked Mr. Kang to give me the money I had entrusted to him in Beijing. As I was putting it into the envelope, I felt that it was quite a large amount. Truthfully, it seemed like an enormous amount to give someone I did not know well and was only meeting for the first time. I divided the money into two envelopes and told Mr. Kang the following.

"If, after having breakfast, I feel like I should give him just one envelope, I'll give him one. But if I feel that I should give him the amount in both envelopes, I'll pass you both envelopes under the table. I'd appreciate it if you could combine the money from the two envelopes together into one."

Then, I put the two envelopes into my coat pocket, and went down to the dining room for breakfast. Mr. Ahn and an elder from the local Korean church were already there waiting.

Over breakfast, Mr. Ahn told me about the 10 years of work he had done as a missionary in China. After listening to him, I let him know that I had heard words in my heart from God for him, while still in Beijing, and had written them down. The words from God included an encouragement about how hard Mr. Ahn was working, what and whom he should guard against, how much the work he was doing pleased the heart of God, and how much God loved him.

After seeing those words, Mr. Ahn was in tears, and told me that although he had been serving God for a long time, it was the first time in his life he was receiving words from God in written form. He was exhausted in mind and body from his work, but after receiving those words from God, he said he felt a supernatural energy course through his body. He felt that he knew exactly what to do next. He assured me that he would work even harder for God's glory.

Give Him All of It

After breakfast, as I was reaching into my coat pocket to give him one envelope, I heard clearly from the Holy Spirit, 'Give him all of it!' I handed both envelopes to Mr. Kang under the table so he could combine them into one. I, then, handed the envelope to Mr. Ahn, telling him that I felt God telling me to give him this gift. He thanked me before we said goodbye. Afterward, I went to a Sunday service at the local Korean church.

As I was leaving the church after service, Mr. Ahn came and found me, telling me that he had something urgent to tell me. So I went to the hotel coffee shop with him, Mr. Kang, and the elder from the Korean church, who we had breakfast with earlier.

In an excited voice, Mr. Ahn told me the following.

"After leaving breakfast, I went back to my place and opened the envelope, and was immediately surprised by the number of $100 bills that I found inside. Last night, I had just visited the local church leaders I have been training for some time. They are now ready to lead churches. They told me that they wanted to form a group and start holding worship services, and asked if I could provide some financial help. But I had nothing to give, so I thought of just giving them another seminar when I see them again tonight. The number of $100 bills in the envelope you gave me is exactly the number of leaders that I will see tonight, so I realized that the money was not meant for me, but given by God to these leaders. I think He wanted to bless and encourage their faith. When I see them tonight, I will tell them everything that has happened today."

I was very moved by his words, and thought to myself, 'What would have happened, if I hadn't been obedient to the Holy Spirit's words, and had only given half the amount?'

Because I had been obedient to God's voice, something miraculous like this had taken place. I do not know what happened in Nanjing afterwards, but I am sure that God used that money in wonderful ways.

Interceding for 300 People Everyday

These days, I intercede for an average of 300 people on a daily basis. The Holy Spirit changes this list in timely ways. Whether someone is placed on the list depends on his or her situation and how much that person needs prayer, and I can learn that by praying for them. Likewise, if I pray and feel that the Holy Spirit is telling me to take a person off the list, I take that person off. In those cases, either there has been plenty of prayer for this person or God no longer needs me to pray for them.

It takes me about an hour to pray for this list of 300 people. In the beginning, it took me much longer, but as a person can learn how to type faster, one can learn how to pray quicker as well. If someone needs more prayer in particular or if someone is in a tough situation, I can pray for five or ten minutes, but most people only need 10-15 seconds of prayer.

It only takes 15-20 seconds to pray the Lord's Prayer that Jesus taught His disciples. Even the Apostle's Creed takes less than thirty seconds to read. It is quite a lot to pray for someone for as long as it takes to read the Apostle's Creed. When you read the Bible closely, there are only a few places in the Bible that contain as lengthy a blessing as the Apostle's Creed.

'Lord, bless this person and his or her children with health. They say they are having trouble with X issue these days, so please help them.'

Praying in this fashion allows me to pray for four to five people in one minute; and within one hour, I can pray for quite a few people. Just as a good batter can consistently hit a ball in the center of the bat, and just as an experienced pitcher can throw a ball into the strike zone time after time, with practice, one can also learn to pray on target. At first, one might throw a few balls, but then gradually, one can throw both balls and strikes. After a while, one can throw strike after strike.

Even after my retirement, I exchanged so many emails with numerous pastors and missionaries that it was difficult to find enough time to sleep. I often stayed up until three o'clock in the morning, reading the messages, praying to God about them, receiving words in my heart from God and then sending them to the recipients. I even thought one day, 'What am I doing? Shouldn't I be praying for myself and my needs instead?'

However, I find tremendous joy in praying for others in this way. If I find urgent messages in my inbox, I cannot help but pray for the people who sent them. I get strength from praying for exhausted and burned out spirits who after receiving their word from God, are in tears, grateful and refreshed with renewed strength.

For a long time now, I have stopped sending Christmas or New Year's greeting cards. I also seldom participate in social gatherings. I made these decisions because I believe that the best way to maintain relationships with people is to pray for them. I have so many things to pray for that, even though I am retired, I do not have much leisure time. Nonetheless, I find immense pleasure and joy in spending time with the Holy Spirit through prayer.

Pray and You Will Not Suffer Disgrace or Shame

Once, when I was sharing my testimony, I said more than I had meant to say, as people kept asking me for more stories. I tend to watch my words in large gatherings, but in this meeting with about 10 people, I spoke a lot more than I had intended.

As I was leaving the meeting, one missionary, I did not know, gave me a piece of paper, saying that he felt the Holy Spirit give him a few words of Scripture, and told him to give them to me. Then he said, one of them was for me.

As I sat in the car, I opened the piece of paper on which several Bible passages were written. As I looked up each one that was listed, I was stunned to find one that said, "Do not boast." In giving several verses to the missionary, and then including among them a word for me, God had spoken to me without embarrassing me. When I returned home, I knelt in front of God, in repentance and thanksgiving. Those who pray do not suffer disgrace or shame, no matter what.

In the depths of people's hearts lies the desire not to be disrespected or humiliated. Even if I do not have money, fame, or power, if I had the respect of others, I would feel like I lacked nothing. Most people are afraid of being disrespected and embarrassed. This is why so many people pour tremendous energy into acquiring large houses, expensive cars, and designer clothes. This is also why people plan and put a lot of effort into sending their children to reputable schools.

When people depend only on other people's opinions of themselves for their self-worth, it usually only takes an instance to be humiliated or put to shame, no matter how much money, power, or fame they might have.

When we read the Psalms, we find that those who fear the Lord will never be disappointed, while those who disrespect God and the people of God will suffer shame.

> They cried to you and were saved; in you they trusted and were not disappointed. (Psalm 22:5)

> No one whose hope is in you will ever be put to shame, but they will be put to shame who are treacherous without excuse. (Psalm 25:3)

All of us are sinners. Who is without sin in this world? The difference is in whether God will cover that sin or expose it. Even if we sin, as long as we confess and repent it, God will not bring the world's attention to that sin and will spare us from shame.

> Blessed is he whose transgressions are forgiven, whose sins are covered. (Psalm 32:1)

Chapter 6

Living As an Ambassador of God

The three dreams I had in life have now all been fulfilled and I only have the desire to serve God for the rest of my life. While serving as the Ambassador, I will be representing Korea, but I will also work as an Ambassador for God.

Praying with God's Heart

In December 2004, I invited Director-General Yeh (Minister-level) to the Ambassador's residence. He was the head of the National Bureau of Religion, the office overseeing all religious activity in China. Accompanying the Minister were the heads of the Christian, Catholic, Buddhist, and Confucian departments.

While hosting dinner, I did not bring up the subject of religion. I knew they prepared an elaborate response if I were to broach the subject. During dinner, we conversed about different topics. All along, I was waiting for a natural opening.

During one exchange, Minister Yeh asked me,

"Among all of the things that you do daily, what do you consider to be your most important work?"

This was the opening I was waiting for.

I replied, "For me, prayer is my most important work."

"Prayer? What is prayer?" he asked.

"It is talking to God and having a conversation with Him while on my knees," I replied.

"What do you pray about?" he asked.

"Most of the time, I talk about difficult work matters and ask for His help. Have you ever prayed before?"

"No."

"So that means you've never prayed for China's leader, such as General Secretary Hu Jintao, Chairman Wu Bangguo, or Premier Wen Jiabao?" I asked.

"No."

I told him, "I pray every day for all the key leaders and also for my friends in China."

He asked, somewhat dubiously, "Why would the Korean Ambassador pray for our leaders?"

I explained, "God loves everyone. The leaders of China probably have many difficult issues to resolve and need guidance and wisdom. I call on God, who loves these leaders, and ask that they would be able to handle these challenging matters well. Since China is Korea's neighbor, China's security and prosperity is important to Korea as well. So I pray that China's leaders would lead a prosperous and secure China."

I continued. "Koreans want China's security and prosperity; we do not want China in chaos. So even if Koreans practice religion in China, you need not worry that it would endanger China. As I have been given this opportunity to meet you, could I ask you for three things?

First, among Koreans living in China, many of them are Christians, and they worship God every week in a public service. However, most of these Korean churches in China do not have official permits from the Chinese government to meet, and so they attend these services with some anxiety. I would like to ask you to grant official permits to these Korean churches in China to gather and worship.

Secondly, the Korean churches are renting halls in hotels and other places to hold their worship services, but because the rental fees are so high, they are suffering financially. I would like to ask that they be able to use spaces that have lower rent or be given some piece of land in places such as Qingdao City, Yanbian Autonomous Prefecture or in a similar area, so that they can construct buildings for worship.

Thirdly, I would like to ask you to issue official visas to the pastors of the churches who have obtained official permits from the Chinese government."

After listening quietly, Minister Yeh answered, "As the two countries have grown in relationship with each other, the number of Koreans residing in China has increased. Accordingly, I think China has a responsibility to make appropriate and needed accommodations for Koreans residing within our borders. When I return to my office, I will look into your requests. As a general practice, China allows the religious activities of foreigners, but often needs to make adjustments to our policies from time to time. We do not want to harm our relationship with Korea because of issues related to religion. So please convey to the Koreans our position. And please ask them not to try to convert the Chinese people. If the Koreans want to gather for worship services only for themselves, we will issue the official permits."

We talked about these issues throughout the rest of dinner. I also told him about how the Korean government, the Korean Embassy, and Koreans responded when China was suffering from the SARS virus, and how God had shown Himself to us throughout the entire ordeal.

The meeting with Minister Yeh that day made an impression on him about how important China was to Korea, how much Koreans loved the Chinese people, and how I prayed for not only the Chinese leaders but for my Chinese friends as well. It was a pivotal point in which the Korean churches and missionaries were able to gain a wider scope of activity in China.

Korea's Ambassador, God's Ambassador

Reading the emails sent by the pastors who serve in churches in China often brings tears to my eyes. They are very alone as they perform God's work in a foreign land. In such a situation, my ability to do anything to ease their burden was a huge blessing to me.

For example, on the first Sunday after starting my work as the Ambassador to China, I went to the Beijing 21st Century Church to worship. Senior Pastor Park Tae-Yun welcomed me warmly and introduced me to the congregants, asking me to say a few words to them.

I told them the following, "When I left China in 1995, I told you that I would be returning within 10 years to greet you as the Ambassador to China. God is faithful and returned me to this land, before those 10 years were up. The three dreams I had in life have now all been fulfilled and I only have the desire to serve God for the rest of my life. While serving as the Ambassador, I will be representing Korea, but I will also work as an Ambassador for God."

For six and a half years, since the day I began my work as the Ambassador, I was able to work with many pastors and missionaries who served in China. I gave my best effort as the Ambassador of Korea, but also as an Ambassador of God. I did this because I knew that it was one of the reasons why God gave me the opportunity to be in China. During that time, I received much help from the Consul Generals and other staff members at the Consular Office, and I will always be deeply indebted to them for their dedication and support.

Spiritual Birthplace

The Beijing 21st Century Church was founded in 1993, right after the establishment of official diplomatic relations between China and Korea. It is one of the oldest Korean churches in China and Senior Pastor Park Tae-Yun served at the church since its founding.

When I first went to China in early February 1992, there were no Korean churches. Instead, a few wives from among the Embassy staff members held Sunday school in one of their apartments. As the relationship between the two countries developed rapidly and as the number of Korean Christians in China increased, they started to hold Tuesday worship meetings as well. That became the foundation on which the Beijing 21st Century Church was established in 1993. My wife and children attended the church since its founding, and I began to go at beginning of the fall in 1994.

Pastor Park has had a special relationship with our family throughout the years we were there. As I have written in an earlier chapter, I received the baptism of the Holy Spirit in January 1995, when Pastor Park baptized me with water. So in effect, Beijing 21st Century Church is my spiritual birthplace. And on the last Sunday, before I left Beijing to return to Korea, Pastor Park asked me to say a few words to the congregants where I first shared about my desire to return to China within 10 years as the Korean Ambassador to China. That very speech was what led many people in the congregation to intercede for me during those years and I believe my ambassadorship was in part a result of their prayers.

In China, any meeting where more than 50 people are gathered requires an official permit. Since the Beijing 21st Century Church was one of the largest Korean churches in China, it always received special scrutiny from the Chinese public security. This resulted in the restriction of many of the church's activities, and I tried my best to help the church and Pastor Park during my time there.

Applauding the Security Guards

Each year, Beijing 21st Century Church organized a gathering for KOSTA (Korean Students All Nations) China. The gathering regularly attracted several hundred students, sometimes over a thousand students, and was closely watched by the Chinese public security.

In the beginning of 2003, for five consecutive years, I participated in KOSTA China as the first speaker on opening day. In September 2003, when I arrived for my talk, I found Pastor Park and other organizers waiting anxiously for my arrival.

As soon as Pastor Park saw me, he spoke in a panic, "Last night, the local security detail and the officials from the religion department came to us, saying that we were not allowed to have a religious gathering. They threatened to close down the meeting if we conducted religious activities. So we promised that we would continue the meeting but that we would not talk about Jesus or God or sing praise songs. So please be aware of this and not mention anything overtly religious during your talk."

I told them I understood and prayed for a bit. And then I went up to the podium and the first thing I said was, "Good afternoon, I am a follower of Jesus and believe in God."

I continued,"I love China and have been studying about China since 1965, when I was a Chinese literature major in college. I have also been praying for China and its people for a long time. Of course, I include in my prayers Chinese leaders such as General Secretary Hu Jintao, Chairman Wu Bangguo, and Premier Wen Jiabao, and I also pray for all of my friends in China. They know that I do this, and are thankful for my prayers. However, when I visit the provinces or the countryside, those who do not know that the Korean Ambassador to China loves China and prays for it daily, often misunderstand my intentions."

The local police officers were sitting in the front row with interpreters, straining to hear what I was saying. I talked about them next.

"Those security officials who are sitting in the front are not like those in the countryside who would misunderstand my intentions.

They are also probably thankful that I love and pray to God for China every day. Everyone, please join me in encouraging and thanking them with a warm round of applause."

As soon as I finished saying those words, all 600 students in the audience gave a loud shout and applauded the policemen. Then, I continued to speak for an hour, speaking about God and Jesus, making sure to lead the audience in applauding the security officials from time to time.

As I was on the way to the Embassy after the speech, Pastor Park called me. "Hallelujah!" he said. "After you finished speaking, all of the security officials left!" The gathering was held successfully in the absence of the officials.

There was another similar incident during the 2007 KOSTA China gathering. When the church registered the meeting with the local authorities, they had reported a potential audience of several hundreds, but once the meeting began, they realized they actually had over 1,200 attendees. Alarmed by the increase in numbers, the local security officers demanded that the number of students be reduced. The students had come from all across China, including many from distant provinces, asking them to return by bus and train without attending the event was simply out of the question.

I called the Consul General and the police attaché in the Embassy and asked them to go immediately and persuade the local security authorities to concede their request. In their flawless Chinese and a deep knowledge of Chinese culture and the concerns of the Chinese government, the Consul General and the police attaché explained the situation to the authorities. Under the condition that the Korean Embassy would hold itself responsible for anything that happened during the meeting, the security officials conceded.

In this matter and in others, God always kept us safe and enabled us to meet and give Him glory whenever we decided to gather with those who love Him.

My Sanctuary

Located across the street from Beijing 21st Century Church is the Beijing International Christian Fellowship (BICF), an international church composed of Christians from over 60 countries. Once, BICF hosted a forum about North Korea. Intercessors and missionaries from over 30 countries, who were praying for North Korea and North Koreans, gathered together. The Beijing 21st Century Church had a close relationship with BICF, so the BICF representatives approached Pastor Park to find an expert on North Korea who could give a lecture to the gathering. In return, Pastor Park asked me if I could be that expert, emphasizing the significance of the forum.

I went to the forum and spoke about how much South Koreans

love North Korea, and how we pray for North Korea. I also explained how the South Korean government received North Korean defectors and how the Holy Spirit was working in those situations. As soon as I finished, the entire audience stood up and applauded me. Many people came to me and told me how moved they were by what I had said, and thanked me. Pastor Park also expressed his gratitude repeatedly, saying how much the relationship between the two churches had grown closer.

The Beijing 21st Century Church was my spiritual sanctuary during my two tours of duty, all nine years and six months, in China. Humble and faithful, Pastor Park is someone I love deeply and for whom I have been praying for daily, even after I left China. My prayer is that Beijing 21st Century Church would continue to be a place of love and fellowship, moving forward boldly as it faces the many challenges that come with representing Korean churches in China. I am confident that they will leave a rich legacy in the history of the Korean church in China.

A God of Consolation and Love

Shandong Province, one of the biggest provinces in China with a population of 93 million, has the closest relationship with Korea. There are over 10,000 Korean businesses in Shandong and among them, the city of Qingdao alone is home to over 4,000 Korean companies. Koreans number about 70,000 in this city. For this reason, the Korean government decided to locate its Consulate offices not in Shandong's capital city of Jinan, but in Qingdao.

I had many occasions to visit Qingdao and Shandong on official business. One of my trips took place in June 2004. After my official meetings were over, I met the Senior Pastor of the Qingdao Korean Church, Pastor Cho Kwan-Shik for the first time. As the head of the oldest and largest Korean church in Qingdao, Pastor Cho's good reputation as one of the most powerful preachers in China preceded him, and I was very pleased to have the opportunity to meet and talk with him. During our conversation, he invited me to be the guest speaker at the worship service the following day. Not being prepared, I declined, but Pastor Cho continued to insist, so I agreed.

After the visit, I began to intercede for Pastor Cho. One day, as I was praying for him, I sensed that he was going through a difficult time. I called him that night and asked whether anything was the matter. He told me that he had been suffering from laryngitis for several days. The next day, he sent the following email to me:

> "I was very touched and encouraged by your phone call and email that came out of the blue. I can't help but praise God for it. As a matter of fact, I was having a difficult time, spiritually

and physically, for the past two to three weeks, but with your prayer and phone call, I was reaffirmed in God's love for me once more, and received God's assurance about my calling and work. Thank you so much for remembering me and interceding for people like me."

I felt that God really loved Pastor Cho. Whenever the Pastor was going through a rough time and needed strength, God let me know. I would then call the Pastor and encourage him.

A Terribly Difficult Time

I led a large contingent of over 200 people from Korea on a visit to Jinan, the capital city of Shandong Province, in July 12-14, 2007. It was for the annual "Korea-China Friendship Week" sponsored by the Korean Embassy. The celebration normally took place in the capital city, so it was uncommon for us to visit other cities during that time. However, that year, the Consul General in Qingdao entreated us for visit, even if it was brief, so we included a short trip to the city on our agenda.

After arriving in Qingdao, we finished all our official business with the city government that day. I was going to deliver a special message at the Chung-Yang Korean Church the following morning, and the only thing left to do was to return to Beijing. However, that night, Mr. Kang Hyung-Shik, who was the consul at the Consulate General in Qingdao, relayed a request from Pastor Cho for me to come and be a guest speaker at his church, the Qingdao Korean Church, the following morning.

I told him that I had previously told another church that I would visit them the next morning. Given that I had already visited Qingdao Korean Church on a previous visit, I asked for his understanding for not being able to speak there this time. Mr. Kang came back to me, saying that in spite of my message, Pastor Cho was pleading again for even a short visit during their first service at 9 a.m. I told him to let Pastor Cho know that I would pray about the matter and would inform him of my decision.

I knelt and prayed for Pastor Cho and the church. God told me to visit the church and also gave me some words in my heart to relay to Pastor Cho. I prepared those words until late into the night and then went to bed.

Early the next morning, I asked Mr. Kang to let Pastor Cho know that I would go to his church, and went to deliver the message. After I took a group photo with the church elders, I passed the note I had prepared to Pastor Cho and asked, "This is why you asked me to come, right?"

Immediately after, I left to go speak at the next church, Chung-Yang Church, and did not find out about what happened afterwards until after my retirement in 2009, when Pastor Cho sent an email about the situation that had occurred in 2007.

A Letter from Qingdao

The Qingdao Korean Church was established 17 years ago by three faithful families. Over the years, it has grown into a mid-sized church of over 1,000 members and 800 youth. Then in 2007, the church went through a crisis. In April of that year, a Korean mega-church organized a seminar about the Holy Spirit in Qingdao. Over 100 Korean pastors were in attendance. On the second day of the seminar, Chinese security police entered the assembly without warning, and stopped the gathering, telling us that it was an illegal gathering without a permit. The Korean pastors were all forced to return to Korea.

On the basis that I helped to organize this "illegal" gathering, I was summoned to various local government agencies handling this matter, and was given a stern warning. Afterwards, incidents that hindered the day-to-day operation of the church took place frequently, and internal disputes arose dividing the church. Exhausted from handling the strife, I felt that I could not continue to lead the church. Thinking that leaving was in the best interest of the church, I began praying specifically about this issue.

I prayed, "Lord, I am having a terribly difficult time. I cannot continue my work for you in this situation. If you think that it is best that I leave this church, please send me a sign by the end of July. If I do not hear from you either way, I will take it as a sign that it is okay for me to leave this church."

I prayed every morning in tears and waited for God's guidance. If God did not speak to me, my intention was to leave China without regrets or second thoughts. Then, I heard that Ambassador Kim was going to give a special message at Chung-Yang Korean Church on July 14. I began to wonder whether God might have something to say to me, given that the Ambassador was visiting Qingdao unexpectedly.

I asked Consul Kang for the Ambassador's presence at my church and was notified the following early morning that the Ambassador would be coming. In my loneliness and exhaustion, I was especially joyful at the prospect of his visit.

When the Ambassador came to our first service, he talked about his experiences in intercession while serving as the representative of the Korean government in China. When he said in the message, "It is truly difficult to hold a church together in China, so the church should do its best to become one body, with the pastor at its center," I was especially encouraged and strengthened, along with the congregants. After the service, when I opened the envelope that the Ambassador gave me, I found the following words from God:

My beloved servant,

I know that you are having an especially difficult time right now.

You are exhausted in body and mind.

It has been difficult for you to do your work there.

I know that you want to leave that place,

but you should stop thinking that way.

You say it's difficult for you right now,

but compared to what I suffered on the cross, it is little.

So be encouraged, and strengthen your heart and mind.

Many things will happen to you in the coming days.

However, as long as you remain in prayer,

nothing bad will happen to you. So do not worry.

You feel tortured in your mind by people who hate and despise you,

but continue to pray, and love and bless them.

Then, they will be ashamed of what they are doing to you.

Good things will happen to you,

and things that you have been praying for will come to pass.

You also will be able to do the things

that you have wanted to do for a long time.

However, be careful.

There are many who attack and hate you, so always be vigilant.

Sometimes your pride can wound others, so remain humble.

Then, people will not be able to attack you.

Be humble, and I will keep you and protect you.

I do not know how much I cried while reading these words from God. I was just asking for a sign, but God gave me amazing words of wisdom and encouragement through the Ambassador. 'I know that you want to leave that place, but you should stop thinking that way.' These were the words that I wanted to hear from Him. Could I have gotten a clearer and more specific answer to my prayer? It was a message of grace from God that instantly threw off the heavy burden and anxiety that I had been carrying on my shoulders for days. It lit again the fire of my faith and assured me of my calling to lead the church. It was as though God and the Ambassador had been watching everything and had heard my prayers.

After reading those words between services, I went into the second service and confessed to the congregation all of the agony and hurt I had been hiding in my heart. Then I read aloud the letter from the Ambassador to the church. As they heard the contents, they found hope and strength in the message from God, and the church became a flood of tears.

Afterwards, I regained my peace in God and have been working tirelessly for God, under his grace. It is not as though the work is without difficulty, but with the command to 'be humble' and the promise that 'good things will happen to you,' I have been devoted to the church wholeheartedly. With God's grace, we have been able to plant a new church every two years, and now have four churches in Qingdao.

The unexpected visit from the Ambassador to Qingdao revived a church in crisis, and led me to recommit myself to God's work in China. It was a leading from God and a time when He showed His presence to us. I do not think I will ever be able to forget this event.

I will be leaving the letter as a legacy for my daughter, Hannah, who says she wants to be a diplomat and serve God. We will keep it as a family treasure to be passed down through the generations, as a reminder of God's faithful guidance of our family.

I knelt down to pray and give thanks to God, grateful that I was able to be involved in an event that testified to the fact that we serve a Living God, who is active among us. Afterwards, Qingdao Korean Church became one of the leading churches among Korean churches in China. It is definitely a result of the blessing poured upon Pastor Cho, who loves God. I still continue to pray daily for even greater revivals to take place at the church and for Pastor Cho to continue to faithfully and lovingly serve God, living out God's mission and purposes in China.

These Words Describe My Situation Exactly

Pastor Um Gi-Young leads the Korean United Church of Shanghai and is reputed to be one of the best preachers and most spiritually-gifted pastors in both Korea and China. I believe that Pastor Um was able to lead and grow a large church in a spiritual desert like Shanghai, since April 2002, because he is a beloved servant of God.

I began a friendship with Senior Pastor Um in 2004. After meeting him, I felt led by God to continue to intercede for the pastor. Because the church was in a difficult situation on many fronts, I was in constant contact with the pastor and maintained a close relationship with him. There were many hardships for him and the church during that time, but we casted our cares upon God, prayed, and fought the good fight of faith. If Pastor Um was going through a particularly difficult time, God let me know that when I was praying for him. I would then call the pastor in response, doing my best to console him and provide other kinds of help. He would also call me when he was struggling and received comfort in being reminded of God's love for him.

In May 2007, I visited Shanghai to attend the opening ceremony for a conference about providing legal assistance to Korean companies in the city. There, I had the opportunity to meet with those who were active in doing God's work in that region. Pastor Um was at this meeting, and there, he asked me to be the guest speaker at his church that Sunday. Even though I tried to tell him that I was not prepared for that, he continued to insist.

When I returned to the hotel, I prayed. When I felt that God was telling me to give the message on Sunday, I told the pastor that I would, and then shared what God had been doing in my life during the service the next morning.

After visiting the church, I met Pastor Um separately, and gave him the words from God I had received in my heart the night before. The pastor's eyes welled up with tears as he read the words, and told me, "Mr. Ambassador, these words describe my situation exactly." I grabbed his hands in response and told him, "Don't worry. I'll continue to pray."

From that day forward, the Korean United Church of Shanghai increased in numbers and became the crown jewel amongst the Korean churches in China.

At the beginning of May 2009, Pastor Um forwarded me this email.

A Letter from Shanghai

In 2004, Ambassador Kim came to Shanghai on official business and ended up being the guest speaker for our Sunday service. We kept in touch intermittently. When I learned that he would be attending our service in May of 2007, I felt a leading from the Holy Spirit that it would be good to ask him to share his testimony with our congregation. So in spite of his initial and repeated refusal, I implored him, and we were able to listen to his stories of faith. His stories deeply encouraged and challenged our congregation.

I was proud of the fact that the person who represents Korea to China was such a person of deep faith. As the Ambassador shared stories of how God manifested Himself during his days in China, the congregants listened intently, holding their breaths. We had heard these stories described in the news before, but only knew about the facts and not all the prayer or the movement of God that took place behind the scenes. The stories the Ambassador shared gave us chills and moved us profoundly.

The Ambassador wrote in a letter the words he had received from God in his heart while praying for me and for our church. He did this twice. I cannot express in words how much these letters ministered, strengthened and encouraged me. I had been exhausted and on the brink of being burnt out, when the Ambassador gave me the words that let me know how God was so well aware of my pain and dilemma. As those words promised, all of the problems and dilemmas that I had been experiencing then have since been resolved. God worked mightily through the Ambassador's prayers.

The Ambassador was not embarrassed or afraid of saying

that he was a Christian and never shied away from professing his faith in Jesus. Whether he was speaking to high ranking Chinese officials or interviewing with the Chinese media, he always spoke Jesus' name.

The Ambassador was instrumental in creating favorable conditions for Koreans to meet and worship freely in China's major cities. The reason we were able to build a Korean church in Shanghai and worship with freedom was due to the Ambassador's tireless efforts in persuading the Chinese government officials.

Like Daniel, Joseph, Moses, and Nehemiah, the Ambassador has maintained the integrity of his faith for his country and for God. Just as Daniel did not partake in the wine and meat served in the king's palace, the Ambassador did not use human efforts to come into a position of power. Rather, he relied entirely on God, seeking His face, and struggling and praying to do His will.

I still pray daily for Pastor Um and the church in Shanghai. And I wait in expectation for the day I will be able to see him in Shanghai and pray together again. I believe that God will bring great revival to the church and bless it immensely according to the love He has for Pastor Um.

A Church in an Apartment

In May of 2005, the Korea-China Friendship Week ceremonies were held in Chongqing. I led a trade and investment mission and cultural troupe of over 170 people to Chongqing, meeting with the Mayor and the Secretary of the Party. During the ceremonies, I asked the Korean residents whether there was a Korean church in Chongqing. They told me that none existed.

I thought to myself, "How can there not be a church in a place where Koreans are living?" The Representative of the Korean Association in Chongqing approached me and told me quietly, "Actually, there is a Korean church. But because the supervision of the public security police is so stringent, we worship secretly in the home of one of the members of the church."

When I asked where the home was located, they told me that it was in one of the apartment complexes where the Chinese locals lived. I became upset. With hundreds of thousands of Korean living in China, it was the first time I had heard that Koreans had been forced to worship secretly because of the interventions of the local police.

The next day was the welcoming banquet for the Korean delegation hosted by the Mayor (Ministerial level) of Chongqing. He and I were very close, and as the banquet was drawing to a close, he said to me, "You are visiting us with a delegation of 170 people for the development of relations between Chongqing and Korea. This is the first time in Chongqing's history that we were visited by such a large delegation of foreign representatives for the purpose of developing our relationship. I thank you so much for the honor. I would like to do something for you in return. Please let me know if there is anything I can do for you."

It was a great opportunity, so I asked for the following.

"There are hundreds of thousands of Koreans living in China, and there is always a Korean church where Koreans live. For example, there are over 10 churches in Beijing alone. However, I have learned that because of the local police, the Koreans in Chongqing are only able to meet secretly in one of their homes. I would like to ask for your help in having the Korean church be able to meet and worship legally."

The Mayor called over the high ranking official who was in charge of religious affairs for the city government, who happened to be sitting at the same table. When the Mayor asked whether there was a Korean church in Chongqing, the official told him no. When told that there was a church, the official said that he knew the city well and that it was not the case. I asked the Representative of the Korean Association to explain where the church was located. When he did, the official replied that a church could not possibly exist in an apartment complex where Chinese citizens lived.

I explained that the Koreans had been worshipping secretly

there and asked him for help so they could gather legally. The Mayor instructed the official to investigate the matter closely and then to assist the Koreans in any way that he could. I again requested the Mayor and the official to issue a permit to the Korean church. As I strongly pushed the matter to their attention again, the Mayor assured me not to worry, and then instructed the official once again.

Early the next morning, I visited the apartment complex where the Korean church was held and visited the Korean school there. Even though the facilities and materials for the school were meager, I saw a few teachers teaching Korean to the students. I was deeply moved by their sacrificial and humble service.

Then, I visited the apartment where the worship services were held. As I opened the door to the apartment, I could not help but be surprised at what I found there. There was a large podium and stage, seating for 60-70 people, and a wonderfully large worship hall. The pastor in charge was on a trip to Korea, and only his wife and about 10 elders and deacons were gathered. I explained to them the agreement I had reached with the city officials and talked to them before returning to Beijing. Then I began to intercede for the church in Chongqing. A month after my visit, Pastor Chung Sun-Gyo, who had been away during my visit, sent me the following email:

"The things that have taken place in the last month or so could not have happened without God's intervention and presence. We are truly thankful that God used you to ignite a big hope in such a small and humble gathering as ours.

On January 4, I went to God during our morning prayer time with the obstacles we had faced in obtaining a permit for the church. I didn't know whether to apply for a permit immediately or to wait, so I prayed daily to God, "Lord, please take care of the situation and send someone to resolve this issue so that no matter who looks or listens to our situation, they would know that it was only by Your doing." Then, when I returned from Korea to hear that you had visited the church, I knew that God had heard my prayers and that all of these things were His work. I was thankful that God was able to use you as a messenger to us."

Afterwards, I began to communicate with this pastor whom I had not even met. In a subsequent email, he said that another surprising miracle happened, saying that an anonymous donor made a donation to build an altar. Then, they were able to purchase a building. But most importantly, they received an official permit from the city government for the church. The process of obtaining the permit was full of interesting stories.

Miracle of the Altar

The Korean Church of Chongqing was able to obtain the necessary permits on January 23, 2006, just two months after they submitted the application. It was a miracle, in every respect. In April of that year, I was able to meet Pastor Chung, face to face, for the first time, while visiting Chongqing during an official trip. He was tall and radiated warmth. Pastor Chung had a dignified and generous demeanor. I shared many stories with him while driving around Chongqing. I was deeply touched by the stories he told about his love for God and the sacrifices he had made while serving Him, and was inspired by his vision for future work. I felt that the church's health and well-being were in large part due to his tear-filled prayers.

In April 2009, Pastor Chung wrote the following words about the events we experienced together.

A Letter from Chongqing

In May of 2005, I was participating in an annual meeting for pastors in Korea, when I received a call from China. The caller told me that our church would be receiving an official permit to hold services from the city government.

"What?" I asked, stunned. "But we haven't even applied for one. How did we get one?"

The caller told me that Ambassador Kim had visited and spoke with the Mayor of Chongqing about the permit and received his authorization. The caller assured me that I would learn more details when I returned to China.

I could not understand how it could have happened. I had never met Ambassador Kim before, nor did I exchange any conversations with him. The issue with the permit was something that I had been praying for since the beginning of the year, but did not share with others, given the delicate nature of the subject. I had heard that submitting an application would open up the possibility of receiving an official permit to meet, but was also afraid that if the timing of the submission was bad, we might just end up notifying the authorities about our location and have to give up meeting altogether. Stuck, I had been wavering about what to do, fearing that either option, submitting or not submitting the application, could lead to disastrous results for our church.

I learned more about the Ambassador's involvement in the issue once I returned to China. A few days later, the city government contacted us and we turned in the paperwork, and we received the permit within two months. This was an extremely rare occurrence in China.

In everything, though, I gave thanks to a God who had been so generous and gracious to a modest church like ours. And I was thankful for the Ambassador's love for God and His church. With the official issue of the permit, we were able to procure a small but beautiful worship space. I ascribe this event entirely to God's grace.

As I found out later, God had initiated the relationship between the Ambassador and our church. When one of the Ambassador's sisters and her friends were visiting Beijing, their faith was revived because of the Ambassador. One of the people in the group talked for hours about the Ambassador to one of the elders in Hong Kong, who was a steadfast intercessor for me. The elder didn't know the Ambassador at all, but after hearing the stories about him, was deeply impressed by his faith.

The next day, the elder was surprised to hear another story about the Ambassador as I was on the phone with her, talking about the story about the church permit. She felt that the two events were not just coincidence and felt the Spirit move within her. When I asked the elder for prayer about the church's location, she shared the concern with her Bible study group members. As she did so, one of the members was profoundly moved by the Spirit to help build a church in Chongqing. Soon after, I received a phone call stating that the member would help fund the purchase of our church building.

We had been praying as a church specifically for a worship

space, and we were able to obtain a beautiful building for our church in time to submit the address of the location in our application for the official permit. There is only one explanation for all that happened: God was intervening on our behalf in even the smallest details.

Chongqing is a large city, but the Koreans only number about two to three hundred. So there was a limit to our church's growth. Because of this, I had always thought that it would be impossible for me to be a successful pastor, if success were to be measured by the worldly measure of the number of congregants one led. But the words that the Ambassador gave to me during the dedication of our new church building were a challenge to me specifically in that regard. It seemed as though he had read my mind. "Victory in fighting the good fight of faith rather than success" the topic of his talk, and all of the words he spoke and the stories he told were on the same theme, and addressed my worries directly.

It may seem that "victory" and "success" are synonymous in some ways, but "success" is used more often in the world and "victory" is used more often in the context of missions. Given the difference, the greatest victory for me would be to serve faithfully in what God has called me to do, which is to pastor the Korean Church of Chongqing. I further understood that God was most pleased and blessed by my work, and with that understanding, a dark cloud of my ambivalence about whether my work in ministry had any value in His Kingdom lifted.

Even though it has been more than seven years since I visited Chongqing, I still pray for Pastor Chung and his church, thinking of his sacrifice and love for God. I especially pray that the dreams that Pastor Chung has for God's work would come to pass.

God Who Protects the Church

In September 2002, I visited Xian in Shaanxi Province. I arrived on a Sunday, so I visited the local Korean church and found about 50 congregants, mostly composed of university students, worshipping with the pastor.

Pastor Choi Yun-Cheol told me that it was also his first worship service in Xian, having arrived just the day before. Given that the church was held in a restaurant, it was the first time in my life I worshipped at a table that was used for grilling Korean barbeque. I felt empathy for the pastor and the church and continued to pray for them after I returned to Beijing.

Three years later, I was able to visit the city again. As I was working out my schedule with the provincial government, I notified them that since I would be arriving on a Sunday, I would worship at the Korean Church of Xian. The government officials disapproved of the idea, telling me not to go to the church because the neighborhood was not a place suitable for an Ambassador to visit. However, I insisted and went straight to the church from the airport.

The church was located in a desolate place. The church that began in a restaurant had grown, but their neighborhood remained poor. The pastor and the 150 congregants were very excited by my visit, and I encouraged them by advising them to love China and the Chinese people. Over lunch, I heard their difficulties caused mainly by the local police and their relentless intrusions. I returned to the hotel with a heavy heart.

The next day, after a series of ceremonies and meetings, I participated in the welcoming banquet after meeting the provincial government's Party Secretary. The Secretary was my age, and we were very close; we even had lunch together at my residence in Beijing. I told him about the struggles facing the local Korean church. I told him about the restrictions they had in their religious activities. I reminded him of how the Chinese living abroad made it a point to meet regularly to build friendships, and asked him to have the city government acknowledge and allow Koreans to meet freely and worship regularly.

The Party Secretary gladly agreed to help. "We have no problem with Koreans meeting by themselves to worship. I will instruct the relevant city government department to allow them to gather without hindrance," he told me. I asked for him to designate one person and told him that that I would immediately put that person in touch with the pastor of the Korean church.

The Party Secretary agreed, and designated a staff member. I asked that official to talk further with me once the banquet was over. I also instructed my aide to contact Pastor Choi and ask him to come to the banquet hall at once. After the banquet, I met Pastor Choi with the designated official and reconfirmed the commitment they had made earlier. I wished them well in finding a common solution to the issue and left. Pastor Choi gave me a call afterwards, saying how he had been able to explain the church's situation to them, and then received the promise of their help. I then returned to Beijing.

A few days later when I was looking at some paperwork, I felt the Holy Spirit prompt me to give Pastor Choi a call. After many rings, he answered with a strained voice.

I asked him, "Pastor Choi, is there someone with you right now?"

"Yes," he replied.

"Is it a Chinese person?" I asked.

"Yes. The official from the provincial government," he said.

"Let me speak to him," I requested.

The person who came on the phone was the same official I had spoken with earlier. I could easily tell that he was flustered. I told him that I was thankful that he had arrived in person to make sure that what he had promised would be carried out quickly. I also told him that I would talk about their cooperation and helpfulness in the matter when I spoke to the Party Secretary next. Although still flustered, he told me that he understood. After I encouraged the pastor to continue his work, I hung up. Several hours later, the pastor sent me an email with the following words:

> "The provincial government officials came to the church today. They told us that they had already known about our existence, and if the Korean Ambassador had not mentioned the issue with the church permit, they were planning on coming with the police in about a month. They began to mention various legal codes and began to criticize the church for violating the laws. It was then that I received your call, and I cannot say enough about your divine timing."

I fell to my knees after reading the email, thanking God for keeping us as the apple of his eye, shielding us from harm.

Prayers of the Pastor's Wife

In 2007, I visited Xian again to participate in the opening ceremonies for the Korean Consulate General in Xian, and went to the celebratory luncheon. Before leaving Beijing, I had some words from God in my heart to convey to Pastor Choi, but the content was such that I hesitated in offering them to him. So I just exchanged pleasantries with him in the reception room next to the luncheon hall and did not give him the words.

Pastor Choi left first to go to the luncheon hall and I followed a few minutes later, but I found him standing just outside the door waiting for me. Thinking that he might be waiting for the words I recieved from God, I reached into my pocket and gave them to him, asking if that was what he was waiting for. He answered yes, received them gladly and walked into the room after thanking me. Shortly after, I received the following email from him:

> "You have no idea how encouraging the words from God were to us. We are so thankful. Astoundingly, the words and sighs of lament that my wife had been writing in her prayer journal for two months were some of the same words that you wrote in the prayer. The day I was supposed to meet you, my wife had been praying that God would send a message to me through you. She told me that you had some words for me, so I had

been waiting outside the door to receive them."

We continued to communicate with each other through email and by phone, and prayed about the various issues that came up for him and his church. We also continued to give praise to God, without whom we would not have been able to resolve the issues that faced us.

Spirit-filled Pastor

Pastor Choi returned to Korea in June 2009, after finishing his six-year work in China well. Before his return, he wrote the following summary about the ways in which we worked together.

A Letter from Xian

On the first Saturday in September 2002, I boarded the plane to China to assume my position as a Senior Pastor. I was to be the founding pastor for the Korean Church of Xian. About 50 college students were in attendance that first week. Among the small number of older congregants, there were a few visitors - the Ambassador, his wife, and their delegation. It felt to me as though God had sent them as angels to encourage me.

Afterwards, the Ambassador continued to intercede for me

and the church and always asked about us via phone and mutual acquaintances. At the time, we had not yet received the permit, and when we heard stories about missionaries being kicked out of China and the hardships experienced by the Korean church in China, we couldn't help but be afraid. In such circumstances, the Ambassador's interest in us and his encouragement gave us strength.

I also received much comfort personally from the Ambassador. More than anything, he was faithful in prayer for me and my church. I know that it wasn't because I was a great pastor, but because he knew that Xian Korean Church would play an important role in God's Kingdom in the future.

The Ambassador also shared with us the words he received for us while praying. To be honest, my theological leanings and my spiritual background led me to consider receiving and acting in spiritual gifts as taboo. I was so thankful that the Ambassador being fully aware of my reluctance, respected and accommodated me.

At first, I was taken aback at how the Ambassador believed so much in the Holy Spirit. But I began to think whether I should seek the Holy Spirit as well, if someone like the Ambassador, whom I deeply respected, was so moved by Him. I also wondered if I needed that kind of gift and the ability to be sensitive to the Holy Spirit. Soon, I started to crave that close, personal relationship with the Holy Spirit as well. Later, God transformed me and my wife into people who sought the Holy Spirit at all times. No doubt, it was the Ambassador who played a pivotal role in this transformation.

The Ambassador also warmly welcomed me whenever he saw me. Of course, there must be many Christian workers who were also treated hospitably by him, but the Ambassador considered us "God's servants called to a barren land" and respected workers like us. I believe it was only possible because he believed that God called him to be the Ambassador to China and because he was so faithful to God.

Pastor Choi sowed many seeds of faith in Xian for God. Who can imagine how many tears he shed and how many prayers he prayed! I firmly trust that God loves him and that He is very pleased with the pastor's work.

I know that because the pastor is someone who longs to be sensitive to the Holy Spirit, he would never do anything without first asking the Lord. I also believe that he is an intercessor who prays for God's Kingdom, and that he is preparing on bended knees for Jesus' coming return.

Go to Nanjing

In the spring of 2005, God kept prodding me to go to Nanjing. And in April, I received an invitation to attend the opening ceremony of a large factory that belonged to a Korean conglomerate. Nanjing is the capital city of Jiangsu Province and I knew the Party Secretary of Jiangsu Province well. So when I contacted the provincial government, he suggested that we have dinner together. However, when I arrived in Nanjing, I found out that the banquet had been rescheduled into a luncheon for the next day. I wondered why the schedule had been changed, but went to give a lecture to the Chinese students at Nanjing University anyway.

There were hundreds of students at the lecture, and among the college crowd, a gentleman wearing a tie stood out; he looked like a Chinese professor. After the lecture was over and I finished taking photos with the students, I found the man standing next to my car. I asked him in Chinese whether he was a professor at Nanjing University. In Korean, he replied that he was Pastor Park Hoon-Suh, the Senior Pastor for the Korean United Church of Nanjing. When I asked him why he was there, he replied that he had come to see me. I invited him to come visit me at the hotel after dinner.

When he came, he began to share his story.

"For many years, I have been ministering in Nanjing. We had a lot of difficulty because the provincial police would try to disrupt our efforts and we could not find a place for worship. When I met the Korean United Church of Shanghai's Pastor Um Gi-Young last year, I told him about our troubles. He told me about you and said, 'If Ambassador Kim was ever to come to Nanjing, he can help you.' So since that day, I have been praying daily for you to come."

As I listened, I realized why God had urged me to come to Nanjing repeatedly. In an excited tone, the pastor continued to speak.

"A few days ago, I happened to be passing by Nanjing University when I saw the notice for your lecture taking place there today. I was surprised and decided that no matter what, I would attend the lecture and find a way to talk to you."

When I heard those words, I realized why the dinner that had been planned with the Party Secretary of Jiangsu Province had been rescheduled. The pastor asked me to make a request to the provincial and city government officials to allow Koreans to worship freely. Then, he added one more request.

"I would also like to request your help for one more thing. Every morning, the wives of three Korean businessmen who work in Nanjing have been praying in tears that their husbands would return to God. Please help us recruit these husbands so that they agree to attend the 'School for Fathers' workshop we are planning to hold at the church."

I was a little taken aback by the request and wondered aloud to him, how I would be able to help him regarding his second request. He told me that he trusted that I would be able to help. After he and the elder of the church left, I prayed later that night about the two requests. I felt assured in my prayers that God would help me on both counts.

The next day, I attended the luncheon hosted by the Party Secretary. As the luncheon was ending, the Party Secretary asked me whether there was anything special that he could help me with. I told him that because of the interventions by the public security police whenever Korean Christians living in Jiangsu Province gathered to worship, they were facing a lot of difficulty. I asked him for his help so that Korean Christians could meet freely, without any fear of persecution. The Party Secretary answered that as long as the Koreans did not evangelize to the Chinese, it was a nonissue for the Koreans to engage in religious activities.

I assured him that I was concerned only with helping the Korean students and expatriates worship freely and repeated my request for the assistance of the provincial government. He instructed the designated high ranking official to look into the matter of issuing a permit for the church.

God Takes Care of Everything

That afternoon the opening ceremony of the factory took place. Nanjing City's Party Secretary had also attended the ceremony, so I approached him to ask for his cooperation with the permit issue for the Korean church as well. He also promised he would help. I, then, asked the same of the Mayor of Nanjing and the city government officials whom I saw at the banquet that night. They also wholeheartedly promised their assistance. It seemed that the permit issue for the church was fast coming to be resolved. Then, there was the second request of helping the Korean businessmen attend the workshop for fathers. I continued to mull over the issue.

When I arrived at the banquet hall that night, there were hundreds of people. During the banquet, a gentleman approached our table and introduced himself to me. He was the head of the company where the three fathers, whom Pastor Park had mentioned earlier, worked. When the head expressed his regret at not being able to host me and offered his assistance with anything I needed, I asked whether I could ask him for a favor. I named the three fathers and asked whether he knew them. He answered that they were his employees. I told him that while I did not want to go into the details, I wondered whether he would ask them to go to the parenting workshop for fathers on the weekends at the church. I explained to him what the workshop entailed and received his consent.

The next day, when I arrived back in Beijing, I received a call on my cell phone.

"Mr. Ambassador! Hallelujah!"

It was Pastor Park. He relayed that all three men had agreed to come to the parenting workshop at the church. We were able to experience God who answers all our prayers faithfully.

I continued to be in communication with Pastor Park over the issue of the church permit. On January 20, 2006, they had finally received a permit. The next day, Pastor Park sent me the following email:

> "Hallelujah! I want to join you in praising God! We received a permit yesterday. They say it is the first permit for religious activity to be issued in the province. I can't help but be moved every time I see the church's name on the permit and the content of the permit which allows religious activity. Perhaps the Israelites experienced something like this when they recovered the Ark of the Covenant. Thank you so much for all your help. Last week, I read your email aloud to the entire congregation. Everyone said 'Amen' to what you heard from God in prayer. Now that the burden has been lifted off of us, we will go forward with strength. I look forward to being in touch with you

again with even better news."

A while later Pastor Park returned to Korea and he began another church in a city called Gunsan, aimed at ministering to ethnic Korean youth and students from China studying in Korea. I still pray for this man who gave his 30s to China and remained faithful to this new calling in his 40s.

The Kingdom Belongs to Those Who Take it By Force

Beijing Church of Praise is small in size but very passionate in their faith. Their Senior Pastor, Ahn Hong-Gyi, was a former bodybuilder and Mr. Korea. He also had a lot of experience as a businessman. Despite his colorful background, I was surprised to see how pure he was in heart.

In June 2006, I attended their 3rd anniversary celebration and gave a guest lecture. After the worship service, Pastor Ahn told me that he wanted to speak in tongues and asked me to pray for him. I told him that it was awkward to do so when there were so many people present. Instead, I told him that I would pray for him every day.

I prayed for him to receive the gift of tongues for several

months, and one day, I suddenly felt an overwhelming sense of joy and began to give God praise while praying for him. I was sure that the pastor had received the gift of tongues, so I called him. He told me that he felt that he had been speaking in tongues for a while, but confessed that he did not know for sure. He asked many questions. As he learned to speak in tongues, he became a prayer warrior, praying for four to five hours a day.

We continued to communicate over email, and at the time of writing this book, we had exchanged over 120 messages. Whenever something happened to him or his church, he would ask me for intercessory prayer.

Once, he asked me for prayer because he had intense pain in his ear. Even though I was busy, I prayed for his healing, and learned later that he had been healed. It was surprising. I was reminded that the Kingdom of Heaven is advanced by those that take it by force. (Matthew 11:12)

The pastor visited the Embassy in September 2007. As we had tea in the reception room, he shared with me the stories of hardship he experienced while ministering in China. I consoled him and said, "Pastor, we have very little in common but whenever I pray, God tells me to pray for you." At those words, tears welled in his eyes.

I continued. "Pastor, please boldly do anything that you want to do in Beijing. God is with you and I am supporting you, so don't worry. Minister as you please."

Touched by these words, the pastor said in response, "When I hear your words, I believe I don't have anything to fear in this world. Though there have been many trials, I am only thankful that I had the opportunity to pastor in Beijing. Who is as blessed as I am to have God minister to my exhausted and burdened spirit and mind so personally through you?"

The pastor ministered in China for seven years and left in December 2009 for a year-long sabbatical to the United States. Before he left, he sent the following email to me and many others, describing what had happened between us during the time we knew one another.

A Letter from Beijing

Unlike many others, I entered seminary later in life, after worshipping God from many different parts of the world and through many different situations. I received the call to ministry while giving over 1,000 testimonies to different audiences. I graduated from seminary in 2001, and just two months after being ordained at the headquarters of the Reformed Presbyterian Church of Korea, I began Korean Praise Church in Guobin Hotel, located in Chaoyang District in Beijing.

Given the short time it took me to become a pastor, there were so many things that I lacked. Even though I began my pastoral ministry at 46 years of age, I did not lag behind anyone in passion. For three years, I put in a tremendous amount of effort, but found many faults within myself. I regretted most, the lack of time I had in devotion to prayer. After we started the church, we began to pray every morning with the congregants, but even as the pastor, I couldn't engage in the kind of deep prayer I wanted.

In the midst of my worries, I heard Ambassador Kim speak at our 3rd anniversary worship service. After the ceremony, I had the opportunity to have lunch with the Ambassador, accompanied by a few others from our church. The topic of our conversation was prayer. Moved and challenged by the fact that the Ambassador himself prayed for many hours, I told him that I wanted to pray deeply, in the Spirit, in tongues, but that I did not have the gift of tongues. Unexpectedly, the Ambassador told me that I could pray in tongues, so I responded by asking him to put his hands on me and pray for me so that I could be baptized with the Holy Spirit. The Ambassador told me, however, that he would pray when he returned home and that I would be able to receive the gift of tongues.

With that prompting, I began to plead with God for the gift of tongues. Even at the risk of embarrassing myself, I even asked for prayer from my congregants. But even as days and weeks passed, I could not pray in tongues. One day, seeing how hard I was trying, the church members surrounded me and began to pray together for me. As I was making all kinds of efforts, I received a phone call from the Ambassador. "Pastor, you seem to be praying in tongues these days," he said. Joyful, I asked him whether what I was speaking was tongues. Just like that, as I received his congratulatory phone call, I began to pray in tongues. I was transformed from being a weak and needy shepherd to a prayer warrior.

Afterwards, whenever I experienced difficulty in the church or had personal requests, the Ambassador sent words that he had received from God for me, via email or telephone. With those prayers and words of encouragement, I was able to overcome and avoid many difficulties. The Ambassador ministered not only to me but to the whole church. He was an amazing Ambassador of Korea, but in his role as an Ambassador of God, he was absolutely precious to those of us serving His Kingdom here on earth.

Pastor Ahn is a faithful servant of God and His beloved son. In the midst of unspeakable difficulties, he only relied on God to move forward. I know that God will continue to love the pastor and bless him thirty, sixty and one hundredfold. I believe that he is continuing his work for God in a way that is most suitable and pleasing in God's eyes.

Chapter 7

The Blessings That Come From Obedience

I still drive this car that stops on the road every once in a while, waiting to hear from God about purchasing a new car. I am sure that God delights in my obedience.

True Blessings From Heaven

I have been a public servant for the past 36 years. In the last 30 years as a diplomat, I have been the Senior Secretary to the President for Foreign Policy and National Security, the Ambassador to China, and the Minister of Unification. In the eyes of many, I have been successful in my career. When people ask me for the secret to my success, I always reply that everything that I have accomplished is due to God's hand over my life; these successes are not from anything that I have done.

Most people want success in one form or another. Some people want to make a lot of money, some people desire fame, and others crave power. To obtain these things, people study hard to get into the best schools, attend meeting after meeting, go drinking, play golf, and generally invest much energy and time to extend their social networks with people of influence.

As someone who has held high positions in government, I have had the opportunity to meet many people who have fame, power, and money, but they all seemed to have something in common;

they were anxious, frustrated, and lacked peace. Due to their own desires to achieve their goals quickly, they often cannot stand to see others succeed. So they easily become jealous and do not have much love or time for others.

Money, fame and power might be signs of worldly success, but if these achievements are coupled with anxiety and ill-will toward one another, they are hardly blessings. Without respect and love, life would be meaningless, even with worldly success. They would neither be counted as success or blessing, but just a chasing after the wind.

In fact, most people in the world depend on others to obtain what they want, so they tend to give special attention to those who are able to help them and place a lot of effort to please them. They also encourage their children to go to good schools so that they too can build this network of potential partners. Those who rely so much on people, however, often find it difficult to rely on God. Perhaps from their perspective, it may seem foolish to trust in a God who may or may not exist, when they can cultivate people into positions of power to assist them.

However, we cannot easily dismiss this phenomenon as only appearing in those who are not Christians. In fact, followers of Christ also often display similar behaviors. Even if they go to church and read the Bible, even Christians find it difficult to meet with God and be assured of His presence, if they are immersed in the ways of the world. Living with a conflicted mind, torn between pleasing Heaven or earth, many often follow their carnal desires, and the opportunities to feel His presence decrease. As a result, many Christians end up walking away from God's blessing, only to pursue the world's definition of success.

In the end, however, there is only disappointment and frustration for those who make people their idols. There is not a single person on earth that will not disappoint us or be able to love us unconditionally. This is because people change with time and circumstance.

> Do not put your trust in princes, in mortal men, who cannot save. When their spirit departs, they return to the ground; on that very day their plans come to nothing. Blessed is he whose help is the God of Jacob, whose hope is in the Lord his God. (Psalm 146:3-5)

For a Christian, true blessing lies not in acquiring money, fame, or power, but in worshiping and living in accordance to His words.

> Humility and the fear of the Lord bring wealth and honor and life. (Proverbs 22:4)

Worshiping God means to ask for wisdom from God and asking wisdom from God means to pray. Riches and honor are God's to give.

> Wealth and honor come from you; you are the ruler of all things. In your hands are strength and power to exalt and give strength to all. (1 Chronicles 29:12)

True blessings come from Jesus and leads to eternal life.

Leaders Must Pray

Many people want to be leaders. Leaders make decisions. People who can make good decisions become great leaders. In important matters, it may take many meetings and compromises before a decision is reached, but ultimately, it is the leader who makes the final call.

Without prayer, decisions are more difficult to make; and without a clear vision, it is difficult to be bold. While I was working as the Ambassador to China, it was boldness that enabled me to tell the President that SARS would be over by the end of June. But it is difficult to be bold with just one's own opinions. I could be bold because I believed I had heard from God in my heart.

The Lord would speak to Moses face to face, as a man speaks with his friend. (Exodus 33:11)

Leaders who cannot win battles find it difficult to receive recognition and love from others. Without being able to properly guide others, it is difficult to be respected. So, if one wants to be a great leader, one must pray. Without prayer, one cannot claim God's power nor have the ability to influence people. Leaders in the Bible like Moses, Joshua, and Daniel were all people who prayed, and it was through their prayers that they were able to find the courage to be bold. Intimacy with God is the foundation on which people can be bold and obtain the potential to be great leaders.

Living Separately from the World

As stated earlier, I lived apart from God for 29 years and then returned to believing in Jesus after my daughter fasted for my return to faith in 1994. With the baptism of the Holy Spirit and through repentance with tears, I was determined to live only in obedience to God's word. With that determination came many things I needed to give up. From someone who used to drink ten glasses of so-called "bomb shots" in one sitting, I became someone who could not even drink a drop of wine. I also began to distance myself from other kinds of worldly pleasures as well.

In every circumstance, I became someone who was determined not to rely on other people but only on God. I also vowed to pray and live only according to His will. As I always had lived, but even more so after I devoted my life to God, I never brought up what positions I wanted to hold and where I wanted to go in my career with anyone. In most cases, I never had to ask anyone for help, because people usually offered even before I asked; but, I also never asked, just in case God would hear those words leave my lips and depart from me. Sometimes I would even become angry when others even suggested that I turn to people for help, because I feared that God would overhear the suggestion.

With a long service in government also came many criticisms and insults from others, but I always blessed those who judged me and prayed for them. Even when newspaper articles harshly criticized me, I never tried to contact the writers. If the criticisms were about my public decisions and conduct, I responded officially, but never made justifications to the criticisms that were directed at me personally. I also never requested cooperation or support from anyone. In every case of offense, I blessed and prayed for the offender.

When I was the Ambassador, people would make derogatory comments about the fact that I did not golf or drink. If I received these peoples' words from the world's point of view, they would be right to judge me. However, I did not think playing golf and drinking were parts of my job description when I was working for my country and people. Even without playing golf and drinking, I held the position of Ambassador to China longer than anyone else. No matter what the criticism was behind my back, God protected and honored me.

When I was the Minister of Unification, people also criticized me for not working but praying all the time. These critics had never been a Cabinet member nor did they know the difficulty of working a day in this position. More importantly, they had no idea what a blessing it was for them to have a Minister who prayed for his country and its people, in spite of the heavy workload.

I never responded to these criticisms because I really wanted to live and act differently from the rest of the world. I also meditated frequently on the words from Psalm 2:

> Why do the nations conspire and the peoples plot in vain? The kings of the earth take their stand and the rulers gather together against the Lord and against his Anointed One. "Let us break their chains," they say, "and throw off their fetters." The One enthroned in heaven laughs; the Lord scoffs at them. (Psalm 2:1-4)

The secret to being victorious over the threats and temptations posed by the world is to live in the world but not be a part of it. When others would describe the insults directed at me, I would tell them that it was natural that people who deny God's existence would criticize a man who belonged to God. They thought that I would be threatened by the criticisms, but rather, I prayed for and blessed the people who persecuted me. As a child of God, I did not look to people for assurance.

> The Lord is with me; I will not be afraid. What can man do to me? (Psalm 118:6)

Praying in the Spirit

We are royal priests in the Kingdom of God. Even though we are royalty, we tend to give up this identity and behave like ordinary people, just to obtain a little more money, fame, or power.

We ought to act, speak, and think like royal priests. If we neglect our identity in God and act like people of the world, we can only be their servants.

> But you are a chosen people, a royal priesthood, a holy nation, a people belonging to God, that you may declare the praises of him who called you out of darkness into his wonderful light. (1 Peter 2:9)

People of the world tell Christians that we should not pay much attention to how we live in this world, given that our salvation is assured and we are headed to Heaven. This is a lie. We should live with intention in this world, seeking to bring Heaven on earth. And prayer enables us to live lives that connect Heaven to earth.

I believe that lack of prayer is the reason why many Christians live lives that are indistinguishable from that of others. Even when they pray, they pray with their fleshly desires, not with their spirit.

St. Paul, in 1 Corinthians 3:16 asks, "Don't you know that you yourselves are God's temple and that God's Spirit lives in you?" Because God's Spirit lives within us, we are God's people, but we often pray according to the flesh; and because we pray according to the flesh, we cannot meet God. When we cannot meet with God, we cannot communicate with or hear from God, which prevents us from partnering with Him in carrying out His purposes. When we do not know His purposes, we cannot hear the answers to our prayers; and without answers to our prayers, we become frustrated and begin to resent prayer itself. Ultimately, we give up praying and live by our own selfish desires. Most people have experienced this phenomenon at least once.

> The wind blows wherever it pleases. You hear its sound, but you cannot tell where it comes from or where it is going. So it is with everyone born of the Spirit. (John 3:8)

People who live according to the world live according to their own desires, but those who live in the Spirit moves as He directs.

Most people worry endlessly because they do not know what to do or how to do it. No matter how many meetings they attend and how many times they deliberate over a matter, they may not have an answer, as we are limited in our knowledge as human beings. It is practically impossible for people to foresee the future and make the right decisions. So the logical and understandable reaction is to be anxious.

However, the Holy Spirit is always able to answer us. The one who led the Israelites with a cloud by day and fire by night, is the Holy Spirit. When we rely on him, a life full of surprises begins.

> By day the Lord went ahead of them in a pillar of cloud to guide them on their way and by night in a pillar of fire to give them light, so that they could travel by day or night. (Exodus 13:21)

This is the answer. He is the Alpha and the Omega, the First and the Last, the Beginning and the End, Almighty God who directs each of us with a pillar of fire and cloud. There is only one path that will lead to victory and righteousness.

Obey the Word

When God gives us a word, whether it is through the prayers of spirit-filled people or through the words spoken in a sermon, we must obey His words. Blessings follow us when we act in accordance to His instructions.

However, it is often difficult to follow what we hear, as it often involves letting go of something we hold dear. For example, when I heard from God, in my heart, about how to handle the SARS incident, I could not have done what I did in reaction to His word, if protecting my position as the Ambassador to China was more important to me. But when I was able to give up my attachments and live according to His word, God was able to act through me and protect me.

I still drive an old Korean car which I acquired for my private use in 2001 when I was appointed as the Ambassador to China. According to the regulations, I could acquire a new car and bring it back to Korea once I worked abroad for more than two years. Since the end of 2003, I would pray about whether I should buy a new car, even with specific models in mind, but I never received God's permission to purchase a new car.

I still do not know the reason for this, but since I know how fruitless a man's plans can be, I have not been able to let myself buy a new car. I still drive this car that stops on the road every once in a while, waiting to hear from God about purchasing a new car. I am sure that God delights in my obedience. And even in these and other small things, I make an effort to act according to what I believe I hear from Him.

> If you are willing and obedient, you will eat the best from the land. (Isaiah 1:19)

I Will Choose Your Son-in-Law

I have a daughter and two sons. My daughter currently works for the UNICEF headquarters. Since 2000, when she began her work with UNICEF, she has constantly lived abroad. Due to this working condition, it was difficult for her to meet someone suitable for marriage or to even arrange dates with prospective suitors. As she became older, my wife and I began to worry, but the only thing we could rely on was prayer. Then in 2003, a missionary prayed for us.

'I will choose your son-in-law. Leave everything to me. I will do it. Pray and intercede. I will lead everything and you will know and see what I have done.'

I told my daughter that I believed what my wife and I heard. I told her not to worry as God would choose her husband, but that I would continue to pray that she would meet him and be married by the time she turned 30 years old (at end of March 2006). I said this because I thought that it would be difficult for her to meet a Korean man when she had to continue to work abroad.

My wife and I continued to pray about our daughter's marriage. We, then, heard from her that she would be returning to Seoul from India for a holiday in December 2004. Given how rarely she was in Korea, I thought it was an opportunity and prayed to God that He would show us her future husband while she was in Seoul.

Through joyful praise, I received confirmation to my prayers from God. My daughter ended up meeting a young man while she was in Korea. She called me when I was in Beijing to let me know that they had decided to continue to get to know each other.

In February of 2005, I had the occasion to attend the annual conference for Ambassadors held in Seoul. After the conference, I met the young man, and as soon as I saw my daughter and him walking together toward me, I knew that he would be my future son-in-law. After saying goodbye to him, I told my daughter that I believed that he was the young man that God had chosen for her.

Even after returning to Beijing, my wife and I continued to pray. We received a phone call from our daughter telling us that the young man was the second son in his family, with a brother who was three years older and still single. She relayed that it was his family's wish that his older brother would marry first some time this year and the younger son marry the following year.

I thought that it would not happen this way, given that if they were to marry in the fall of 2006, she would be older than 30 years old, which was different from how I had been praying to God. The issue of their wedding date was a discussion that needed to be had between the two families. However, because my work was in China, I could not easily travel to Korea. So I prayed that God would send the young man's parents to Beijing. A bit later, I received a phone call from his father that he would like to visit us in Beijing at the end of April, given that their children were in a serious relationship. I gave thanks again to God for answering my prayers.

God Keeps His Word

A few days later, I told God that as I had been praying for a long time, my daughter needed to be married by February of 2006 and began to ask Him for a wedding date. While praying, I received confirmation that my daughter would be married at the end of September 2005.

I told my wife to begin preparing for the wedding because our daughter would be married at the end of September. She questioned me, saying we had not even met the parents of the young man. I just told her to start making preparations.

At the end of April, we met his parents in Beijing, and even though we had just met, we talked like old friends. They asked us to understand their desire to see their oldest son marry first and their second son married in September of the following year. We talked about having the engagement ceremony in June. I did not tell them about what I had heard from God in prayer and agreed to their requests.

At the beginning of June, we held a simple engagement ceremony with only our families in attendance. The day before my future in-laws returned to Seoul, I told them the details of how I had been praying for our children's marriage.

"Through prayer, I believe it is God's will that my daughter would be married at the end of September this year. Could you also start to pray about this upon your return to Korea, and if you receive a similar answer from God, move the wedding to September? If you do not receive the same answer, I am fine with having the wedding next fall."

They told us that they would pray and returned to Korea. I told my daughter who was returning to her work in India the next day that if she was obedient to God's word, the wedding would happen, but if she was disobedient, the wedding would not take place. So I advised her to resign and return to Korea.

My daughter agreed and submitted her resignation as soon as she returned to India. I continued to pray that God would move the hearts of my future in-laws. On the night of June 18, I received a strong word and praise that He had answered my prayer. Four days later, I received a phone call from the young man's father, consenting to moving the wedding date to the end of September.

After the phone call, I bowed down to God in thanksgiving. I was so thankful that He had answered the countless ways and times I had prayed for my daughter. I sent the following email to my future in-laws:

> Dear Mr. and Mrs. X,
>
> I was so delighted to receive your phone call on June 22 that you were also in agreement to move the wedding to the end of September. I am also so grateful that in the midst of your circumstances, you considered our requests and prayed through it.
>
> As I told you in detail last time, God told me a month before your visit that the end of September was the best time for the wedding. Of course, we knew that we needed your consent and that we could not make the decision ourselves. Accordingly, I prayed many times whether the other dates you proposed were good, but I continued to receive the word that the end of September was the best time, so I didn't know what else to do. On June 18, while in prayer, I felt that you would agree to the date in September, so I have been waiting to hear from you.
>
> It is so amazing that even before we met you, God gave me faith about the date of the wedding, all the way back in March.

It is even more surprising that everyone came into agreement with that word. How could such things happen? I believe that it was possible because the marriage of our children has been preordained by Him, and a sign that many good things will take place as a result of their union. I believe that more than any other family, theirs will be full of blessing and grace. And I know that the meeting of the two families is just as precious as the meeting of our children, so I continue to thank God and keep all of us in prayer.

Blessings and victory in Christ to you always,
Kim Ha-Joong and Bae Young-Min

A Wedding Without Invitations or Presents

A few days later, I received word from my daughter in India that her supervisor, to whom she submitted her resignation, suggested that she request for leave without pay instead, which was later approved. I, once again, was amazed and thankful to God.

My daughter's wedding was scheduled for September 22. My wife told me that as this was the first wedding in our family, we needed money to prepare for the wedding. I told her to do as she pleased.

Even though I told her such words, I thought that even if we received a small amount of monetary gifts in return for what we had given as gifts at my friends' children's weddings, it would be sufficient to cover the cost of the wedding. However, when I went to God in prayer, I felt that God did not want us to even circulate wedding invitations, much less receive gifts. I was stunned, but more than that, I felt so bad towards my wife. Nevertheless, I could only be obedient to what I heard from God.

I could do this because I was sure that God had ordained our daughter's marriage. I knew that His plans included greater things than receiving what we had given to other couples at their weddings. If by chance, people found out my daughter's wedding, I knew that regardless of whether I wanted to receive gifts or not, people would send them. So we had no other choice, but for my wife to go to Korea by herself and plan the wedding quietly.

God Pays Attention to the Smallest Details

I received a phone call from my wife in mid-August while she was in Korea. We needed to receive the "haum" (a traditional gift box from the groom's family containing gifts for the bride) before the wedding, so it seemed that I should return to Korea by September 16 at the latest. I told her that I would do so and went to God in prayer. He told me that I should not return by September 16. So I prayed with the 17th, 18th, and 19th in mind, but He told me that I should not return on any of those dates, but that I should return to Seoul on the 20th.

I conveyed what I had heard to my wife who responded in anger that she could not possibly do all of the wedding preparations by herself until then. However, I could only be obedient to God.

Then the Chinese Ministry of Foreign Affairs announced on September 8 that the fourth meeting of the Six Party Talks (diplomatic talks regarding North Korean denuclearization among representatives from South Korea, North Korea, United States, China, Japan and Russia) would begin on September 13 onwards in Beijing. Then, I received orders from headquarters in Seoul to prepare for the arrival of Deputy Minister of Foreign Affairs and Trade Song Min-Soon (later Minister of Foreign Affairs and Trade) and the team from South Korea that would be participating in those talks on the 13th.

Then, I realized why I could not leave Beijing until the 20th. And I thought that the reason why I could not leave until the 20th was that the talks would be over on the 19th.

When the representatives arrived, the talks reconvened; but then all of a sudden it was stalled. The Chinese government tried to end the meeting by the 18th, but it ended up being postponed to the 19th. As I already knew what was going to happen, I told Deputy Minister Song to relax. The closing ceremony that was scheduled for the morning of the 19th was postponed until 12 p.m., shortly after the sessions closed with the adoption of the famous "September 19 Joint Statement" (confirming the intent that all parties to the meeting would work to denuclearize the Korean Peninsula).

The next day, I sat next to Deputy Minister Song on the plane and returned to Seoul. That night, we received the "haum" and I attended my daughter's wedding on the 22nd. Since we had not issued wedding invitations and did not notify anyone, there were just a few relatives and close friends in attendance on the bride's side; only a few people from the Ministry of Foreign Affairs and Trade, who had found out about the wedding attended.

The day after the wedding, I took the first plane back to Beijing. Aside from those who oversaw my schedule, no one else in the Embassy knew that my daughter had gotten married and they only found out about the wedding later.

My daughter's wedding was blessed and planned by God from beginning to end. The God who never makes a single mistake allowed me to serve my country faithfully on an important matter and be present at our daughter's wedding. Hallelujah!

The more thankful consequence of our daughter's marriage was that it caused the faith of my wife and daughter to deepen in unimaginable ways. I am still profoundly thankful to God each time I think about my daughter's marriage.

That Woman is Your Daughter-In-Law

I always regretted not living a life of faith earlier and always prayed that my sons would stand more approved in the sight of God sooner. Like most fathers, I had greater expectations for my oldest son. Accordingly, I wanted my daughter-in-law to be someone who would be able to receive the lineage of faith that my wife had received from my mother. So for a long time, while praying for my oldest son, I asked for a daughter-in-law who would fear the Lord, rather than one who had money, power, or fame.

After work in June 2005, my wife told me that she thought our oldest son was in a serious relationship with a young woman. I was curious about this young lady. Until then, I had not paid much attention to who he was dating, but on that particular day, as soon as I heard this, I had the unusual desire to go to God in prayer about the situation. Without saying anything to my wife, I went into my room alone and sought God. When I asked him whether this young woman was suitable for my son, I was startled to receive the direct reply that this woman was my future daughter-in-law. Surprised, I stood up, and then went back on my knees again to thank God for preparing such a woman for my son.

The next day, I prayed again, just to make sure. God gave me the same answer. Then when I prayed morning and night for three weeks in a row and received the same answer, I told my wife. I felt as though I should meet this young woman, so I contacted my son and asked whether her parents would allow her to visit us in Beijing.

A few days later, he said that her parents gave their consent and that they would come to Beijing at the end of July. I continued to pray about their impending visit and met them on July 22.

I asked her to sit next to me and then asked her directly whether she would be my daughter-in-law. “What?” she asked in surprise. I told her that I had prayed about it and that God had told me that she was to be my daughter-in-law. So I told her that if the two of them agreed and her parents also gave them permission, then they had our blessing. She seemed deeply moved. I asked her whether she prayed and whether there was anything she had been asking for deeply in prayer. She told me that she desired the gift of tongues. I told her that we would spend that day in preparation and that we would pray together the next day.

A Daughter-In-Law for the Record Books

The next evening, the four of us - my wife, my son, my future daughter-in-law and I - sat together. Then we began to pray together for the gift of tongues for her. Within a few minutes, she received the gift and she wept as she prayed.

I smiled and told her that she was a daughter-in-law for the record books, given that she had prayed with her father-in-law even before the wedding and then received the gift of tongues. Then I asked her, "What does your father do? What about your siblings?"

Until then, I had not asked my son about her background. I had gone to prayer in less than an hour after I found out that they were dating, and because God had told me then that she was to be my daughter-in-law, I did not feel the need or even have the interest to ask what her parents did, what they were like, or what the rest of her family was like.

After we finished praying, I took her to my study and showed her the notes I had taken while I had been praying for the past month or so. Among them were the notes of thanksgiving I had written while praying twice on the night of June 25, and the following morning, praising God for giving us the kind of daughter-in law we had desired.

I told her that we had decided that she would be our daughter-in-law, without knowing and without desiring to know anything about her, her family, or her parents. This was because God had told us that she was to be our daughter-in-law. I told her that I did not know why He had told me this, but I said that if she were to marry my son, she would need to pray that my son would only serve God, and that she would need to intercede for our whole family to be one that only feared, depended on, and prayed to God. I told her that I believed this was the reason why He had given her to our family. I told her that I did not want anything else from her but only to be someone who would stand firm in her faith, love others, and be one that people of this world could recognize as being from a family of faith. In tears, she told me that she would do so.

> Do not be anxious about anything, but in everything, by prayer and petition, with thanksgiving, present your requests to God. (Philippians 4:6)

The Most Beautiful Wedding

In July of 2006, the two were married. In preparation for the wedding, my wife worried about money, as she did for the wedding of our daughter. In fact, she even told me explicitly to not pray about whether we should or should not receive wedding gifts. I did not answer her and went into my room to pray.

'God, you heard her right? My wife told me not to ask you about this. That's how much we're struggling. This time around, please allow us to receive monetary gifts for the wedding.'

'No, you cannot.'

'Then, would you allow us to send a few invitations just to

those that are close to us?'

'No, you cannot.'

After I ended my prayer, I went to my wife and apologized to her, saying that we again could not receive gifts or send invitations. I told her that I understood that it would be difficult but that she should try her best.

I felt horrible that I could not help my wife financially with the wedding preparations. I even wondered why the Holy Spirit would not allow us to receive gifts for the wedding. The number of Korean companies who were in China were over 40,000. Even if a few of them came with gifts to the wedding of the Ambassador's son, there would be a long line. I felt that taking advantage of my position was not something that a person of faith should do.

My wife again went quietly to Seoul and prepared for the wedding. The night before the wedding, I again did not tell anyone at the office except those in charge of my schedule, and went alone to Seoul.

We had a small ceremony at our church. But the wedding ceremony was set apart and beautiful. The two young people read letters to each other, confessing their love, and when the groom sang a love song to his bride, I was overwhelmed with gratitude and joy. Even though everything was lacking in terms of worldly goods, this wedding ceremony that was full of God's blessing was far more beautiful than any other wedding I had seen. I wept tears of gratefulness in my heart and thanked God.

Nonetheless, I still felt bad for my son. I knew that if we had been open to receiving wedding presents, their life together would have begun with more financial abundance. I felt like being a high ranking government official actually prevented me from being more generous to my son. So I asked God to bless him a hundredfold for the sacrifice my son was making on my behalf.

Later, God did bless my son abundantly. He was able to move to a job that acknowledged his skills and gave him a higher salary. And through my daughter-in-law, he began to be transformed. I give thanks to God who gave us such a woman as our daughter-in-law. With all of my heart, I desire to see my daughter-in-law receive the legacy of our family's faith and pass it on to the next generation.

Can I Feed Her A Banana?

When I was living without faith, I raised my children with human ambition. As I grew in my faith, however, I realized that parents were God's shepherds and that I should not raise my children with worldly ambitions. So I began to pray for my grandchildren even before they were born, and asked God to look after and raise them. I also listened for His purposes as I was praying.

In September of 2005, while my daughter and son-in-law were on their honeymoon, I prayed for them as a couple. But strangely, instead of praying for them, I found myself praying for their child instead. I wondered why God wanted me to pray for their child, but for a year, until the birth of my grandchild, I continued to intercede for her. In January of 2007, while I was praying for my daughter, I received word in my heart that something would happen to her child, and that she should pay attention. I also received word that as long as she prayed for her child, everything would be well.

When I told my daughter about this word that I had received, my daughter told me that nothing in particular was the matter with her child. A short while later though, my granddaughter began to suffer from eczema and food allergies. Even though my daughter took my granddaughter to several different doctors, it could not easily be cured.

In December of 2007, my daughter emailed and asked me if I could pray about how and when it would be appropriate for her to introduce milk, eggs, broccoli, tofu, and strawberries to her daughter. She also added that without feeding her daughter any meat, she would lack iron, and so she wanted to feed her beef. She asked if I could also pray about when it would be appropriate to feed her some beef as well.

With the list that my daughter sent in front of me, I began to pray.

'God, can we feed her some milk?'

'No.'

'What about eggs?'

'No.'

'Broccoli?'

'Yes.'

'What about spinach?'

'Yes.'

'And can we give her some tofu?'

'Yes.'

'Strawberries?'

'Yes.'

'When should we start giving her beef? Can we start in December?'

'No.'

'What about January of next year?'

'No.'

'What about next February?'

'No.'

'March?'

'Yes.'

I sent my daughter an email the next day. "Don't feed her eggs or milk, but everything else is okay to give her. You can start giving her beef in March."

My daughter adjusted the menu according to those directions, and my granddaughter began to improve.

Then, my daughter's work called her family to move to the United States. Even though my granddaughter's eczema was better, it was not yet cured.

In the fall of 2008, during my tenure as the Minister of Unification, I found my wife waiting for me, holding a piece of paper when I returned home after 11 p.m.

"What's on the piece of paper?" I asked.

She told me that our daughter had sent an email containing a new list of fruits and vegetables.

"How can I pray for such a long list?"

As I was taking a shower, I felt God speak to me.

'This is why I told you to pray for your granddaughter before she was conceived.'

I had no choice but to ask my wife for the list and began to pray. As I prayed, I marked the sheet with x's and o's for the fruits and vegetables she listed. My daughter obediently followed the list and my granddaughter's eczema was almost completely gone.

This story might sound crazy to people who do not have faith in God, but I believe that if one prays in love, God answers even the most trivial requests, so that we might experience the grace of a Living God more deeply.

Cultivate Prayers of Faith

While praying, if there is an overwhelming sense of joy, and afterwards, there is a peace that comes upon you, there is a very high chance that those prayers will be answered. Even after praying, if the prayer is about our selfish ambitions and desires or is against God's will, we will continue to wonder whether the prayer will be answered. Also, if we have any unconfessed sin before God, we will not see our prayers answered.

When we pray prayers that will be answered, there is no doubt in our hearts. There is a certainty that what we are praying for will come to pass, and it is easy to continue to pray; however, if there is any doubt, our prayers get stifled. Even if we pray many times, the thought of 'Will this really happen?' will stop us from praying. A prayer that receives an answer is one that is prayed in faith. If we pray in faith, knowing that our prayers will be answered, we can persevere in prayer, even for many years.

> I tell you the truth, if anyone says to this mountain, 'Go, throw yourself into the sea,' and does not doubt in his heart but believes that what he says will happen, it will be done for him. (Mark 11:23)

In November of 2008, I had the opportunity to have dinner with a world-famous intercessor. She asked me whether my mother was still alive. I told her that she had passed away fifteen years ago. She continued to ask me if my mother had been a Christian and had prayed much.

She then asked me whether I felt thankful towards my mother. I told her that while I did not thank her every day, I did thank her whenever I thought of her and on the anniversary of her passing.

The intercessor told me to thank my mother every day. She relayed that it was my mothers' prayers that God had been answering for the past 15 years. And more importantly, she told me that there were even more prayers yet to be answered in the coming years.

The prayers of faith that had been prayed by my mother had led me to become the Senior Secretary for Foreign Policy and National Security to the President, the Ambassador to China for six and a half years, and the Minister of Unification. My mother, the prayer warrior, prayed with the faith that knew her prayers would be answered 15, 20, and even 30 years after her death. Prayers of faith are profoundly significant. Prayers of faith are not easily discouraged. Therefore, we should pray these prayers of faith for our children and for our generations.

Epilogue.

A Life that Follows the Leading of the Holy Spirit

When we as sinners receive Jesus Christ into our hearts as our Lord and Savior, the Holy Spirit comes to live within us. When the Spirit resides within us, we are followers of Jesus. Through the indwelling work of the Holy Spirit, we see God at work, and we confirm and know that God is a Living God. When we pray in the Spirit, God will work through His Spirit.

> So I say, live by the Spirit, and you will not gratify the desires of the sinful nature. (Galatians 5:16)

When the Spirit that lives within me begins to move, I do not need to make any plans. I just need to follow Him as He asks. This is why the lives of people who follow the Holy Spirit become lives of adventure. Others might think that adventures are dangerous, but those who live in the Spirit know that they can withstand any danger, attack, or criticism that come their way.

> You, however, are controlled not by the sinful nature but by the Spirit, if the Spirit of God lives in you. And if anyone does not have the Spirit of Christ, he does not belong to Christ. (Romans 8:9)

Confess Your Sins, Lead a Righteous Life

People of the Spirit are always bold. This is because they already have the answers to their questions. So in all circumstances, they are full of joy and peace. The Spirit of truth has given us freedom and hope. People of the Spirit can also love anyone because the God of love has poured His love upon us first. As a result, people of the Spirit are not anxious in any circumstances, and can always be thankful, bold, forgiving and loving.

How does one become such a person of the Spirit? In living a life of faith, after all these years, I came to the following conclusions:

First, we should confess our sins and cultivate a righteous life. A person of prayer should always have a pure heart, one that distances itself from sin.

Blessed are the pure in heart, for they will see God. (Matthew 5:8)

Although, it is impossible to not sin, we should always try our best to not commit it. But when we do sin, it is so important that we repent before God, confessing our sins and asking for forgiveness. Jesus was crucified on the cross that He might forgive us our sins, through his shed blood, when we run toward Him in repentance. However, if we fear confessing our sins to God and do not pray, we walk away from God and we can no longer pray. We should not fall prey to the schemes of the enemy who does not want us to pray.

You belong to your father, the devil, and you want to carry out your father's desire. He was a murderer from the beginning, not holding to the truth, for there is no truth in him. When he lies, he speaks his native language, for he is a liar and the father of lies. (John 8:44)

Dishonest people cannot pray in the Spirit. How can one lie and then be able to pray the prayers that come from the Father's heart? The Holy Spirit cannot move in such a person.

But why do people struggle with dishonesty? It is because they either do not know that there is a Living God or they know about this Living God in their minds but have no conviction in their hearts. As a result, they live in deception, lying to themselves. They think that perhaps He is alive, but that He could not possibly know everything that they are doing.

Of course, God sees everything. He knows our thoughts and the desires of our hearts.

Love Deeply

The second thing to do is love deeply. God is love. He works when we love others. If there is hatred in our hearts, we cannot pray.

In fact, we do not naturally want to pray, but His love that is poured into our hearts through the Holy Spirit enables us to pray for even those we do not like. So for people who pray, loving others is critical. Those who love can pray, and when they pray, they can love anyone. So those who love well are also those who pray well, and those who pray well are those who love well.

> If I speak in the tongues of men and of angels, but have not love, I am only a resounding gong or a clanging cymbal. If I have the gift of prophecy and can fathom all mysteries and all knowledge, and if I have a faith that can move mountains, but have not love, I am nothing. If I give all I possess to the poor and surrender my body to the flames, but have not love, I gain nothing. (1 Corinthians 13:1-3)

Even with deep faith, if we lack love, we have no power. Love is the basis for all intercession. It is only when we are overflowing with love for others that we are able to pray for them. God is blessed when we pray in tears, not for ourselves, but for others. If we love our neighbors like ourselves, we can pray daily for 300 people and pray 10,000 times over a period of 19 years. There is no way that God would not answer prayers that are sown in tears and love for others. If we prayed for someone 10,000 times, who in the world would refuse to answer those prayers?

We should love others deeply and forgive others seventy times seven as Jesus commanded. If it is for those we love, we should pray up to 10,000 times. Do not try to persuade someone without praying for them in tears. The thought that we can move others with money or gifts is a thought that is derived from our flesh. What is the use of praying for 40 days or 400 days, if we are full of criticism and envy of others?

No matter what someone says, we must love. Even when people judge and dislike us, we must still love. In my case, when I pray prayers to forgive and bless those who slander me, I can only pray for a few days before the prayers stop. The Holy Spirit tells me that I have prayed enough, and that I need not do so any longer. It is because I was victorious in love. There is nothing more important than truly loving others. No matter who insults or criticizes us, if we in turn bless them and love them, we can defeat any schemes of the devil.

I believe that one of the reasons why I was able to become the Ambassador to China was because I had a deep love for China and the Chinese people. Love is power, and prayers of love can release miracles.

Focus Only on God

Thirdly, we must pray in accordance to His will. When I pray not for my benefit but for His will, God hears my prayers.

"God, please send our child to a good university."

"God, please give us a bigger apartment."

"God, please promote my husband at work."

If everyone prays these kinds of prayers, which ones should God answer? If we pray for a bigger apartment or a good university for our children, we probably could not even pray a hundred times before we stop. We cannot pray persistently for our own desires; however, if we pray for our country or our neighbors, we can pray tens of thousands of times. It is difficult, though, to see God answer prayers that were made to fulfill our own worldly ambitions, and accomplish our own goals for our own gain.

We need to stop thinking about our fleshly desires and only focus on God. If we want to become better at praying in the Spirit, we need to simplify our lives. If we can discard the excess that clutters our thoughts, distractions are reduced and praying becomes easier. It is fruitless and greedy to think that we would immediately be able to pray in the Spirit when our minds are focused on worldly ambitions throughout the day.

> The sinful mind is hostile to God. It does not submit to God's law, nor can it do so. Those controlled by the sinful nature cannot please God. (Romans 8:7-8)

When I pray, I do not think about other things. This is possible because all I do is pray and work. If I watched television dramas, movies, and sports, it would be difficult for me to focus on God. But I have no memories of such distractions in my mind when I pray. I only know my work and study, and prayer. I do not know much else.

Meet God Face to Face

Lastly, we need to meet God face to face. We should never use prayer to move God on our behalf, but rather, meet with Him in conversation. That is how we receive answers to our prayers. Remember that God always loves us and is always waiting for us.

There are many who live how they want and then go to God in desperation when situations arise. 'God, help me! I really need your help!'

Sometimes these prayers are answered, but this is not what God wants from us. If He is always alive within us, how can we only call on Him when we are desperate?

Others only seek God for specific things. They even go on retreats to pray these prayers. 'God, should I begin this business or not?'

Even if one prays for hours, it is difficult to hear from God when one is only seeking God for what they need. This is different from always being with God and then asking Him about His thoughts on starting a business. If we do not surrender the things we need to let go of and do not obey God, but only look to His hands more than desire to see His face, we are using God. Most of the time, people who pray these prayers end up falling asleep, without understanding or hearing anything from God.

'I need to get this request answered soon. . .' Such people are only interested in receiving solutions to their requests.

'What in the world is He saying?' Even if such people want to hear from God, they do not understand Him.

Being able to hear the Holy Spirit is not an ability or a gift. If the Holy Spirit lives within us, we are able to hear Him. It is nothing special. Many people want to receive the gift of prophecy, but the best thing to do is to truly love people and spend time talking and listening to God.

The Purpose of Those Who Live By the Spirit

People of the Spirit have a purpose. We have to be in the forefront, not only to transform ourselves but our cities and the nations. We cannot fight the forces of evil in the world with just one on one evangelism. Of course, each soul is precious, but if the person who becomes a believer continues to go back to their old ways of living, they will have no impact on society. Transformation needs to happen at the cultural and social levels. People of the Spirit need to participate in all aspects of society and proactively transform the nation and its people.

We need to proclaim God's truth to a world that is continually tossed in the waves of sin. Only those who walk by the Spirit will be able to accomplish this task. I began to think about what I believe to be the purpose of those who are led by the Spirit.

First, we must emphasize the importance of repentance and honesty. Our society is mired with lies and wrongful actions. Even churches are full of self-help messages about obtaining worldly success and not in obtaining victory in Christ.

In such a time as this, should not the church be proclaiming the message of the cross for those that are living unrepentant lives? Should we not proclaim the love of God that forgives and redeems us?

We also need to seek His will, not our own. Many Christians are seeking their own success and gain. Many churches are also seeking the glory of man, not the glory of God. One of the things that Jesus hated the most was making the church a marketplace, and these days, we often see the church operating as a business. We need people who will boldly call these situations out.

Lastly, people of the Spirit should pray for the unification of the Korean peninsula. The relationship between North and South Korea is not good right now. However, we should acknowledge that we are headed toward unification and that it will take place according to His will. We should pray in repentance and tears. As people who are living in the only divided nation on earth, we have a calling to know the heart of God who waits for our prayers.

As I wrote before, people of the Spirit have the duty to not only pray for individual people but for the transformation of a society. We should keep in mind that God always has His eyes on us. Therefore, we should not look to the world, but to God to prepare for the return of Christ. We should also act in courage and truth, as people of the Spirit, not only for the sake of our present generation but for future generations to come.